FINDING
GRACIE

FINDING GRACIE

A Memoir

GRACE PAPAGNO

iUniverse®

FINDING GRACIE
A MEMOIR

iUniverse books may be ordered through booksellers or by contacting:

iUniverse
1663 Liberty Drive
Bloomington, IN 47403
www.iuniverse.com
1-800-Authors (1-800-288-4677)

ISBN: 978-1-4917-9388-6 (sc)
ISBN: 978-1-4917-9391-6 (e)

Library of Congress Control Number: 2016906885

Print information available on the last page.

iUniverse rev. date: 05/02/2016

DEDICATION

For Stephanie, who gave me the opportunity to grow up all over again, happily.

CONTENTS

PREFACE

I was brought up in the small, sweet town of Lindenhurst by hard-working, middle class parents, in a house that was solid and structurally without flaws. There were none of the hideous problems that made their way to the movie screen: no excessive drinking, no spousal abuse, no talk of hatred for any other people. We were considered an average American family. They were the 1950s, the days of fountain pens and soda fountains, junk drawers and rag-bags, clothes-lines and hand-washed dishes.

But beyond the facade of the sweet times and bustling family, beyond the chatter of voices throughout the house and beyond my understanding, secrets lay untold, quietly coexisting in our day-to-day lives.

I can remember as a little girl hearing about how much I was loved. The evidence, I was told by Mom, was all around me: I was fed good food three times a day, there was a solid roof over my head, and I had clothes to wear. The good sisters at school reiterated those sentiments, admonishing me and all of my classmates to thank God each day for our good fortune. I had, though, a difficult time trying to reconcile the words I heard with the emotions I felt. Mom never kissed or hugged me or my sisters, but she did have a steadfast rule that any of her children coming in or going out of the house had to kiss the cheek she presented. She didn't listen to my stories from school, nor did she have any interest in what I thought about things. My role was to do well in class, to stay out of trouble, to do my chores, and to make my family look good.

Mom was always in a hurry. She cleaned our house quickly and deliberately. She bustled through the grocery store. If she stayed in the car and told me to go into the dry cleaners to pick something up for her, she would honk the horn for me to hurry, even though I was not dawdling. She made me fret, and I was embarrassed in front of the other customers and the shop owner. When all her children were enrolled in school, Mom chose to work as a secretary at the town clerk's office, a job she loved to escape to each day. At dinner, the family listened to the stories she told of couples who came to her for their marriage licenses, some endearing, others sharply critical of such unfavorable circumstances as premarital pregnancy or interracial union. Carole, the eldest of the four daughters, was entitled to have some say at the table. But by the time Mom had reluctantly given up the spotlight to Carole, it left no time for Bridget, Margaret, or me to speak of our day.

Daddy was pretty quiet in our house. He worked hard in the painting and decorating business that he and his brother, my Uncle Mike, owned when I was little. When his green truck pulled up to the house at 6:30 each evening, my sisters and I would run to greet him with shouts of, "Daddy! Daddy, you're home!" We were strictly taught by Mom not to hang on our father, whose back was "bad," and so he would lean down to kiss each of us before going into the garage to wash his brushes and skin with the benzene he kept there. Daddy never lifted nor carried any of his daughters for fear of aggravating his bad back.

Many times when Mom brought the four of us girls shopping with her, she would leave us in the car. I remember once she parked in front of EJ Korvettes "for just a little while." What seemed like hours passed and little Margaret, known to us as Margie, began to cry. The car was warm so Carole said we could roll down the windows a little. We waited and wondered if one of us should venture into the store to find Mom. Had she forgotten about us? Eventually she returned with her purchases and told us we were being silly, complaining about waiting for her. She made it clear that we would have been too much trouble to take through the store.

Mom did love to cook, and she made wonderful meals for us. It was through her cooking and baking that Mom demonstrated her love. It was no wonder then, that her children became hearty eaters, a quality considered healthy in the fifties. I suppose that it was because I was so active that I did not become overweight. Slowly, each of my sisters and I took in all the love that we could, substituting Mom's dinners for hugs and her cookies for kisses.

Mom bestowed upon each of her daughters an attribute she saw fitting. Carole was the smart one, I the pretty one, Bridget the athlete, and Margie, well, Mom's joke was that there was nothing left for Margie. Mom also paired us in bedrooms according to our ages. Carole and I shared a room, even though she had little interest in me because she was the eldest, a birthright that lent her an air of authority and superiority. Bridget and Margie shared a room, giving them the opportunity to develop friendship and remain so throughout their lives. I became a loner in my own home.

And so my stories begin, the memories of my life growing up. These are vignettes—short tales of both good and bad times in a bygone world. They are my stories. I have, with the help of a few excellent people, changed some very negative patterns that had begun long before I was born. I occasionally mourn the loss of that simpler world, but I would not return to it. The woman I have become no longer belongs there.

You'll find these vignettes are not always in chronological order, but are told in the order in which you need to hear them.

SPECIAL THANKS

To my dear friends Linda Pratt and Susan Collins who never lost faith in me.

To Judy Campbell, author, who first suggested that I get serious with my story and find an editor.

To Jennifer Caven who not only edited my book but also lit a fire under me when summer and the beach distracted me.

To Jimmy Ciminelli who kept my old computer working until I completed the entire memoir.

To Len who listened and listened and listened.

FEAR

I GREW UP IN FEAR. It was a way of life then, the means by which countless post-World War II parents kept their children in line and out of trouble. I suppose they learned it from their parents who learned it from their parents and on and on, the "spare the rod and spoil the child" philosophy passed down through the ages. But it seems to me that many of this particular 1940s generation of parents, having saved the world for democracy, felt that breeding fear into their children was their natural right. I can speak only from my own experience and through what I saw in many other children of my time.

My first memory of fear was calling to my mother while she was hanging laundry on the clothes line in our backyard. She was talking with a salesman peddling *The Book of Knowledge Encyclopedia*, which, in fact, she bought from him by saving dimes in a small metal bank he gave her to demonstrate what an economical purchase she was making. I remember her smiling at him, flirting in her way that reminded her and all those around her of her beauty and desirability. How quickly that smile turned into a scowl upon hearing my call. "Don't wake up the baby!" she barked. I remember feeling the twitter of butterflies in my stomach from having committed a punishable infraction. I scurried into the living room and slithered behind Daddy's comfortable upholstered armchair in the corner to hide. I was four years old.

Perhaps because she was distracted by the handsome salesman,

Mom had apparently forgotten me by the time she entered the house. Baby Bridget had not awakened, so after a safe amount of time, I crept out of my hiding spot, careful to avoid Mom lest she remember my crime and punish me with a "spanking," a euphemism for a severe and relentless beating. I still recall relief at having averted a nasty morning.

It's funny how I have always remembered Margie, born five years after me, as the center of the most terrifying scene I'd known. I remember Carole's being very brave for a little girl. It must have been when I was seven years old and Carole nine. Bridget was a long and lean four-year-old and Margie was the "baby," having just turned two that month. I remember Mom's tirade about Margie's not being a baby anymore. It was time for her to give up her baby blanket. I knew there was going to be big trouble when Mom's voice became shrill and her black eyebrows rose to a scary point. None of us kids had any idea where this episode would take us when, strangely, Mom marched us down the basement stairway and turned us to the right into the furnace room, instead of to the left where the television and couch were. There we little girls stood, lined up while Mom announced, "This is what happens to baby blankets!" She tore the comfort object out of Margie's tiny grasp, opened the furnace door and let us stare into the box of flames. I could feel the heat radiating on my face. Mom took the blanket and hurled it into the inferno while Margie howled in agony and Carole blurted, "You won't get away with this! This is bad! We'll stick together!" Bridget and I stood in terrified silence. I knew the slaps and I knew the belt. Now Mommy had the furnace.

Unfortunately, my faith in Carole as leader of sisters was short-lived. As her means of defense from then on, she chose to side with Mom. She also began having bouts of anxiety, which filled our house with her screams. The method Mom used to quell this situation was to hold Carole's head under the cold water faucet as we others stood by.

I knew other times of fear: spilling milk, arguing with Carole, making a mistake. I learned to say, "I'm sorry" before I knew what, if anything, I'd done wrong. When I entered school at age six, I was warned about the principal's spanking machine and believed it was real. Why wouldn't I? The nuns at school also told us that our mothers were always right and that if we were punished for something we did not do, that we should accept it as payback for some other infraction for which we had escaped punishment.

Daddy worked days, and we children were instructed to make a peaceful home for him at night. He ceded the role of raising his children exclusively to Mom.

As a result, I grew up always trying to fathom the mysteries of right and wrong, fair and unfair, just and unjust. I learned to be self-sufficient. As an adult and then as a single mother, I knew the fear of facing an emergency without the means to overcome or escape from it. I always felt as if I were working "without a net", with no one to help or rescue me in times of trouble. It took me years to observe that whenever I was in dire straits, without money or extended family something always happened, as if by magic, to replenish my resources and allow me to find my way clear of difficulty. Some may call it God's intervention; others say it is chance. I know in my heart that what I call the positive energy of the Universe watches over me, and I need fear nothing and no one. It has taken me half my lifetime to learn not to be afraid. I still have a moment of anxiety when a problem arises, but then I am able to overcome it in an instant. But fear is still my first, though momentary, reaction.

I have grown straightforward and strong. I have ended a cycle, the conclusion of which was long overdue. The proof for me is my daughter Stephanie. She is honest, kind, strong, compassionate, disciplined, intelligent, lovely, and fearless. Since her birth, I have empowered rather than hobbled her. I still keep her baby "blanky" along with other sweet mementos tucked neatly in a box in her closet.

We know the tree by its fruit. I am proud of Stephanie and of myself.

THE CHRISTMAS TREE

THE DAY AFTER THANKSGIVING, my sister and I, like all children we could imagine, were focused on the upcoming most important day of the year—Christmas. Carole was already in the first grade, so she could print her alphabet with ease. I sat next to her at the kitchen table and did my best to scratch out letters, often asking Mom how to make this one or that, and how to string several of them together to form a word. Just a few sentences would suffice to alert Santa to our hearts' desires, and we'd be off to mail these special missives.

One night soon after that, Mom suggested to Daddy that he'd have to go to the attic to pull down the boxes of Christmas decorations. During the day, while Carole was at school and baby Margie was taking her nap, Mom began to make the *strufoli*, Italian honey balls, by rolling and then cutting the dough into small pieces to fry. They would hold until another time when she could drizzle them with honey and sprinkle them with nonpareils.

One night after work, Daddy took the tall ladder off his truck and begrudgingly hung lights around the perimeter of our Cape Cod home. He always rattled off a litany of curses while grappling with the peak of the roof, but as was our way, we neighborhood kids outside pretended not to hear. Christmas was drawing nearer, and we were thrilled with the prospect of brightly colored lights illuminating our neighborhood, special foods and desserts gracing our tables, and presents, oh yes, presents from Santa! Although Carole and I were too young to read a calendar or notice exactly what day of the week it was, we were excitedly aware that the best day of the year was looming nearer, but something was missing. We had not yet put up a Christmas tree. Everyone knows that in order to have Christmas, there *must* be a tree.

After dinner one night, Mom sat at her desk poring over the checkbook. She did this as a monthly ritual, and the task held no interest for anyone else in the house, even when Mom would look up and exclaim, "I found the missing dime. It was lost in the arithmetic. Look, see here where I found it." It was not finding the ten cents that thrilled Mom, but the fact that her checkbook was reconciled perfectly.

This particular night, when she'd finished her checkbook, Mom looked up, said, in a matter-of-fact tone, "Well, there'll be no Christmas tree this year; it doesn't fit into the budget," and walked away. Carole and I were dumbfounded. No Christmas tree? She might have just as easily announced that there was no Santa or that there would be no Christmas. We looked to Daddy, but he just shrugged his shoulders and followed her out of the room.

The spirit of Christmas did not dwell in my house the next few days. The subject of a Christmas tree was closed, and no one contradicted Mom, even about such a critical matter.

On Christmas Eve night, right after dinner, Daddy rose deliberately from the table. "Get your coats on," he ordered Carole and me. We did as he said with questioning faces, wondering where we were going and what we were going to do so late at night. Because it was snowing, we donned hats, gloves, scarves, and boots as well as coats and headed out the door. Daddy took our hands, and we walked up our street the long two blocks to the Montauk Highway. Large white flakes swirled around us. The soft stillness was interrupted only by the squeak of our boots pushing off the snow and our heavy breathing as we stomped the long distance on short, child legs. Carole and I didn't understand why we were stopping at the corner of our street. Daddy pulled at an opening in the snow fence circling the lot. There, Christmas trees, the leftovers that had not been sold, leaned like frozen ghosts under the weight of snow in the abandoned lot.

"Okay, which one shall we take?" Daddy asked.

5

"But Daddy—" Carole began to object.

"How about this one? This looks like a really good tree," Daddy said, as if to himself, while he lifted the Douglas fir and shook it free of its white cloak. "Yeah, this is a really good tree."

Daddy picked it up and hoisted it over the snow fence. Then, lifting its heavy base, he dragged the tree's tip along the sidewalk as we three returned home in the dark, quiet night.

After some time Carole asked timidly, "Daddy, isn't this stealing?" I suppose she feared that we'd committed the sin we'd all learned was inexcusable.

"All those trees are going to be thrown away. No one else wants them. That's not stealing," was his answer.

We spoke no more about our simple crime in the night. I reached up and held onto the hem of Daddy's jacket as we marched home with our purloined tree. I wondered if we had, in fact, stolen it. But I thought there must be times when stealing wasn't really a sin, and that there were more than two sides to right and wrong. When I saw the expression on my dad's face, I knew I was right in this very important matter.

MY OLD GANG

"SOMEONE'S AT THE DOOR. Go see who it is," Mom commanded without turning away from the venetian blinds she was vigorously dusting. I hadn't heard a knock but headed obediently for the door.

It was Barbara from next door. She stood outside our kitchen, her red hair glowing, even though clouds hid the sun. She handed me a small object which, when I looked at it, was actually a folded up piece of lined paper that had been mysteriously locked into a wadded up triangle. "Theresa was sick," Barbara began, referring to her older sister. "She's getting better now but can't go outside for another few days. She asked me to give you this."

"Thank you." I stared at this intriguing gift.

"Who is it?" Mom called from the living room.

"I have to go. See you later." Barbara escaped before being subjected to Mom's scrutiny.

"It was just Barbara from next door. She's gone." I worked the paper around in my fingers, unfolding it to discover printing. I handed it up to Mom. "What does it say?

"Oh, Theresa wants you to go to play with her." Without thinking, Mom returned to me the first letter I'd ever received.

"Can I go?"

"Go on. Be home by six o'clock and don't be late!" Mom was very strict about everyone being at the dinner table on time.

7

I'd never played with Theresa. She was two years older than I and in the second grade. Barbara and I had played outside, but now I was going to the Bernat house, by invitation, to play with Theresa *inside.*

It was drizzling out and a bit chilly, but their door was open. Only a screen door protected the interior. I rapped on the wooden door-frame twice, hard. I knew that Connie, Mrs. Bernat, was hard-of-hearing.

Standing over her stove, she turned to see who the visitor might be and said, "Oh hi, Grace, Theresa's inside. She's waiting for you."

Since all the houses on the block had been built identically, I easily made my way through the kitchen, smelling unfamiliar food aromas, past the phone nook in the hallway wall, past the bathroom, and the downstairs doorway to the end bedroom. There I found Theresa in her pajamas, sitting on her bed. She smiled and asked, "Did you get my note?"

"Yes, but I can't read it. What does it say?" I offered her the creased paper. Slowly, she helped me sound out the words: *Do you want to play Tic-Tac-Toe with me?*

We must have played for well over an hour and then moved on to play Connect the Dots. At five to six, I said my goodbyes and darted home. It had been fun just sitting there on Theresa's bed, each of us holding a pencil with a piece of paper between us. The time evaporated as we laughed and joked while taking turns besting one another at the simple games. I felt like I'd arrived home with a special secret. I smiled at nothing in particular and was calm and undaunted when my sister, Carole, sneered that it was my turn to clear the table and dry the dishes, a situation I ordinarily hated and fought. "Okay," I said cheerfully, and she seemed irritated by my complacency.

When Theresa was fit to return to the outdoors, she came calling for me. We sat for a long time on my back stoop, deciding what we would do that day. "Let's go to the woods," she suggested, her eyes prompting me.

"Yeah!" It was a great idea.

"Okay, I'll be right back." She ran across Mom's lawn and was back in seconds with Barbara.

"Don't walk on the grass!" Mom had poked her head out of the back door long enough to chastise us and then vanished. (We had learned that spinning each other around and freezing into a fallen position, a game called Statue, or simply spinning until we were dizzy and fell down was acceptable on Mom's lawn. Crossing it to travel back and forth was not.)

The woods two doors down were a play land for my old gang. We spent entire days there exploring one section or another. There was a small fallen tree that, when struck with a stick, emitted an army of little red ants that bit us. Even though the little monsters stung, we regularly smacked the trunk and screamed and ran from the prickly pain. Deeper into the woods was a giant tree from which big kids had tied a rope to create a swing seat out of rags. When we were finally big enough to climb that tree, we swung, each of us taking turns. There were, in the center of the woods, thickets that opened up into spaces, giving the illusion of rooms. Some kids had previously brought old linoleum flooring and laid it down in the openings, providing a perfect spot to play House.

Bicycles afforded us new freedoms. We discovered the mud flats near the bay, endless brackish marshlands that froze in wintertime and made for safe skating, as the ice lay upon only a few inches of water. In springtime we caught pollywogs there, brought them home, and watched their miraculous metamorphosis into frogs. We also rode to the island near Montauk Highway where, if we sat long and patiently enough, we would spy muskrats and turtles. We picked punks, what we called cattails, and dried them to "smoke" later on in the autumn.

Our moms always insisted that we return promptly for dinner, but lunchtime was more relaxed. After breakfast, we made ourselves peanut butter and jelly sandwiches, wrapped them in wax paper, placed them in our pockets, and rode off for adventure. One such destination was the abandoned Bulk's Nursery on Montauk Highway in West Babylon. After a ten-minute ride, we hid our bikes in the underbrush and explored the woods that led to the bay. As we neared the water, vegetation became thin. We fed on wild strawberries in June and found wild blueberries in summer. There, on our own private beach, we untied and discarded sneakers, peeled off socks, rolled up dungarees, and walked through the cool water collecting beautiful stones and beach glass, all the while discussing how Captain Kidd's treasure might possibly have been buried right there. As we waited for our feet to dry, we sat on the beach, ate our sandwiches, and plotted to return to dig it up.

We found a bike path that could match any roller coaster ride. All the kids called this thickly wooded area The Jungle. A narrow alley had been worn into it by many tire tracks. The trail was long, winding, and encompassed hills that, when traveled at high speeds, rendered bikes airborne, suspended for a moment or two before plunging back to earth. The thrill was exquisite!

One time, on the first ride of the season, Theresa led the group. I was following close behind when she suddenly began to scream. I blinked and focused my eyes to see hundreds of yellow jackets swarming over her. She had ridden right through their nest. We swatted blindly at the creatures while high-tailing it for home. There, Connie applied mud and kisses to Theresa, who remained out of commission for the remainder of the day.

Snowy winters made biking impossible, so we summoned our imaginations to conjure up new projects. We walked to the far edge of the woods and grabbed handfuls of long, dried grasses, twisting them until they broke off, gathering bundles and bundles of them. We brought these to the Bernat's back yard where we had built the walls of a fort out of plywood boards. We crisscrossed ropes across the top of the fort and wove our grass into a roof. This project took days to complete because we had to trudge through knee-deep snow to get to and from the woods. It was tedious and painful labor, yet we continued with the determination of lost campers in the wilderness. When the fort was finally completed, we took empty coffee cans, poked holes in the tops with a screwdriver, entered the Bernat's basement, opened their furnace and deposited several pieces of burning bituminous coal into each can. Holding the tops of the cans with gloved hands, we were able to transport the warmth to the fort where we placed feet, hands, whatever was cold, near the "heaters."

Rainy days were easy. With roller skates and skate keys in hand, we headed for the Bernat basement where we skated for hours around and around the lally columns that supported the house. When we tired of skating, we let the dust settle and drew a large conch form on the cement floor to play Snail. As in Hop Scotch, we tossed a stone or piece of coal into a drawn box, hopped to it, hopped back, and if we accomplished this successfully, without stepping on any lines or into anyone else's box, we could write our name in that box, claiming it as a private "rest area." Sidewalks were too narrow for Snail, so rainy days were special. It was only on such days that we were allowed to play inside.

My childhood gang dispersed as we grew older, and the adventures we shared slowly evaporated. Game time turned into homework time. Bikes were put aside for boys. Our beloved woods were torn down without a thought for the towering old tree, and an oversized, elaborate house took its place. The mud flats became the site of a new elementary school. The Jungle was turned into a housing development, and the Bernats finished their basement and had a new oil burner put in where the old coal furnace once stood.

The island of turtles and punks endures, unnoticed, a relic of a lost time. It now lies between two shopping centers. The land that was so long ago Bulk's Nursery remains a beautiful woods, although the area south of it, near the bay, is now a sewage facility.

It was a special time, a sacred time for us back in our day. My old gang and I still get together now and then and talk of our long-ago adventures. We laugh and reminisce and sometimes weep.

When my gang was outside playing, we were free. With a peanut butter and jelly sandwich in our pockets and the order to "stay out of trouble and be home by dinner," we could venture out to any one of the many places in our play kingdoms without fear of parental judgment. That was, of course, until six o'clock, dinnertime, when Theresa and Barbara returned to their house full of too many kids and just enough of anything to waste, and I to my world of strangers.

KINDERGARTEN

SWIRLS OF BUS EMISSIONS MADE the damp early morning air bluish. Nausea enveloped me. I sat in the back seat of Mrs. Glasco's car, hesitating while her son Edward stepped onto the curb. "Are you okay, honey?" Mrs. Glasco asked quietly. She lived down the street from me and was friendly with Mom. When school began several months earlier, she and Mom had arranged to drive us kids to kindergarten on alternate days. She prompted me out of the car, and I stood looking at the ominous building they called the Annex. Throngs of children were filing in through the doorway.

"I don't feel so good." I could hear my voice falter. I didn't want to be there. I wanted to be home with my mother. I didn't like the smell here. The sister inside the Annex was scary. She had a scary voice. She yelled. Her clothes were strange. She had a crown of stiff white cloth bound tightly against her forehead. She had scolded me for not putting away the blocks after playing with them, but then she had said, "Line up," and I'd hurried to line up so I would be the obedient child Sister wanted me to be. Big girls from the eighth grade had been assigned to be our monitors while Sister went to the convent to eat her lunch, and the big girls were squealing that a scary spidery-crab-like thing was coming up through the drain into the sink in the little bathroom off the classroom. They said they were trying to push it back down the drain with a stick. I was scared of the spidery-crab. "Grace, are you okay?" Mrs. Glasco almost whispered.

With that, I could feel the salty fluid fill my mouth. I leaned over and vomited into the gutter. Quickly Mrs. Glasco offered me a sweet-smelling tissue from her fragrant handbag. "Oh, dear," she said calmly, "Get back into the car, honey."

I could see that Mom was not pleased when Mrs. Glasco brought me home. You could tell when Mom was angry, because her black eyebrows rose to a peak like those of Sleeping Beauty's stepmother, Maleficent. Mrs. Glasco explained that I had been sick and couldn't go to kindergarten that day. She had apology in her voice and tenderness in her demeanor. "Okay. Thank you, Anita," Mom said. "She'll go to school tomorrow—that's for sure."

Inside the house, Mom became very angry. "Go to your room!" she yelled.

I sat on my bed and whimpered, "But Mommy, I didn't feel good."

"Oh, no. You're not going to start this business! Your sister Carole never had a problem, and I'm not going to start having trouble with you!" was her answer, and she continued her house cleaning. By this time, Mom had worked her way into my bedroom and was furiously dusting my dresser.

"But Mommy, I missed you," I cried. The words of love I tried to express whirled around the room with the displaced dust and fell to the floor.

"You will go to school, and you will not get sick! This is some sort of game you're playing now!" With each word, her fury grew.

"But Mommy, I love you so much," I sobbed as I watched her back.

With that, she opened my top dresser drawer, the one where I kept all my little treasures, and, dusting its inner lip, slammed the drawer on my prized possession—the plastic Santa Claus pin, the one whose nose lit up when I pulled the string, the one that was my souvenir from the circus.

I cried out in pain as I held the smashed pin, and that seemed to make Mom feel a bit better about having her day upset. The remainder of my day was lost in sobs of rejection and wails of mourning. But I learned to hold back nausea and hide fear and, as was Mom's dictate, I attended kindergarten.

✄

Many years later, the day, the one that most moms feel comes out of sync with time, arrived far too soon. My daughter Stephanie was scheduled to begin kindergarten. Her eyes had been especially bright as we laid out her "big girl" school clothes on the bench in her room the previous night. "No, Mommy, *these* socks with *this* dress," she directed until she was satisfied with the results. She was ready for school. Tiny Tots, the nursery school Steph had attended part-time for the past three years, had helped prepare her. The tour of her new school, Sunrise Drive, coupled with our frequent conversations about what to expect in kindergarten and how much fun school would be, helped to assuage any fears Steph might have felt, although I never noticed any. She was ready.

The principal where I taught understood the importance of this occasion, and he'd arranged for a substitute teacher to take my first period English 11 class while I stood with the other mothers on the corner of Greeley Avenue and Bohack Court waiting for the school bus to arrive.

I was not the only mom to hold back tears while our kids boarded the large yellow vehicle, but with a smile and a wave, kisses wafting, I sent my only child off to a new world. Steph sat in a window seat in the middle of the long corridor of rows. She smiled, even laughed, and waved to me, so eager was she to begin her new adventure.

"They weren't supposed to grow up so fast," Lidia Howe observed with a smile. Her Janet sat next to Steph and would join her in Mrs. McAllister's class.

"Oh, Lidia, at this rate I think we're going to snap our fingers and find ourselves sitting at high school graduation," I replied. We both chuckled, our eyes glued to the faces behind the window. The bus door folded shut, the engine roared, and in a cloud of exhaust, the bus lumbered my girl off to school.

That afternoon, when Stephanie arrived home from her first day, her chatter was endless. Oh, how wonderful were Mrs. McAllister and the children and the school. How they played games and learned letters. How Steph had eaten her peanut butter and jelly sandwich and bought milk like a big kid with the money I had put in her little change purse. Life was good, Stephanie felt safe, and I learned the gentle art of reshaping my past through my child's experiences. We loved kindergarten!

CRAYOLAS

LINDA BARON WAS RICH. She had attained this status, in my estimation, not because her parents owned the plot of land behind their house, which extended the Baron property line to the next street. Nor did she hold this enviable condition for any of her possessions—other than her box of 48 Crayolas. Although my box of eight crayons contained every color any six-year-old first grader attending Our Lady of Perpetual Help School needed to fulfill art projects, Linda's box of 48, the largest assortment sold then, came complete with silver, gold, and copper that actually shone. They were magnificent!

Since I sat directly behind her, and because she was generous in nature, we often shared such exotic colors as periwinkle and fuchsia and aquamarine. In this fashion we coexisted amiably for many months until Justin Current ruined everything.

As was the custom in Catholic school in those days, at lunchtime, the good sister in charge of the class would appoint a monitor to sit at her desk in the front of the room to watch over the class and report any infraction such as talking or standing. On this particular day, there seemed to be some confusion, for when Sr. Mary Daniel left us to get lunch at the convent, she seemed to point to Justin as the monitor. Justin was not monitor material. We all knew him to be a "bad boy." Surely there had been some mistake.

Before a moment had passed, Justin, in a fervor of newfound power, stood up and began to walk up and down each aisle, pointing at each student saying, "You're monitor." (Justin may have been naughty, but he certainly wasn't slow.)

By the time I was appointed monitor, all the new little monitors were up, walking around the room, threatening to report the "non-monitors." It was, for a Catholic school classroom, pandemonium. I suppose Justin had decided there were enough helpers to cause havoc and ended his appointments with me. Oh, but Linda wanted to be monitor! She turned to me and pleaded again and again, "Please appoint me monitor."

I sat frozen in my seat. I sensed the "wrongness" of the situation and knew from experience that Sister wasn't going to like this at all. But there was my friend, Linda, begging me to say the few words that would empower her to be in charge. "You can be monitor if you like, but I don't think it's a good idea," I whispered.

With that, she flew away from her desk and, along with the fifteen other six-year-old supervisors, took up her responsibilities.

At that moment, the tall, black-clad Sr. Mary Daniel flung open the door. "What is the meaning of this!" she demanded in a deliberate and threatening tone. The room was instantly a tableau of petrified creatures in mid-movement. You could smell the fear as the miscreants were herded out of our classroom, and we few remaining students sat powerless and terrified for our friends.

After what seemed like hours, slowly, heads downcast, the penitent scoundrels filtered back into the classroom. "What happened?" I whispered to Linda. *Was she well? Had she encountered the infamous "spanking machine" we'd all heard rumors about? Had she seen the principal?*

"Don't speak to me," she sneered and turned her back to me.

When finally Sister appeared at the door, she looked at me and cackled, "And you, young lady, what you did is written all over your face."

The horror of my crime sank in with the shame I was now to bear. The class resumed in blistering silence. I pulled up the tabletop of my desk, found my handkerchief, and tried rubbing out the words that had somehow found their way to my face, proclaiming my guilt. Still hiding behind the desktop, I whispered to the girl seated next to me, "Are there words on my face?"

Even though she assured me that my stigma had been erased, I was only relieved when later I saw my clear skin in the girls' room mirror.

Now that things were back to normal and class had resumed its rhythm, everyone breathed easier. At coloring time, I tapped Linda on her back and asked, "Can I borrow your light pink?"

She whisked her face away from mine, her hair snapping at me. I supposed that now the friendship was over and no fancy colors would ever be forthcoming again. I had to be satisfied with my basic eight from then on.

Forty-five years later on Christmas morning, my daughter Stephanie and I sat in our usual spots on the floor in front of our lighted tree. One gift for Steph, another for Mom. One gift for Steph, another for Mom. "What's this?" I whispered as I recognized the contents of the gaily-wrapped package. "A box of 64 Crayolas with a built-in sharpener! Oh, Steph."

"Mom, now you have the biggest box of crayons made, the ones you should have had in first grade. You deserve them, kid."

My Stephanie is a very wise child.

A RIDE WITH UNCLE KENNY

IT SEEMS TO ME THAT IT was on those rare long and dreary days of summer—the ones for which no plans had been discussed, nor escapades begun, when we kids were sitting on the front steps of the Bernat house wondering what to do—that Uncle Kenny would arrive. Although his presence promised adventure, Uncle Kenny was no knight in shining armor riding a gallant steed.

This simple man, the uncle to my neighbor buddies, Barbara and Theresa, piloted his old, sputtering pickup truck down our street and into view. I think we heard his arrival before we saw him. His hair was windblown and gray, and his wrinkled, leathery face covered with shiny white stubble.

He tossed us a wave, slowly slid off the ripped cloth-covered seat, and emerged in front of the house. He was average in height, stooped a bit by advanced years, even though now I figure him to have been only about sixty years old. His body was the relic of a once-strong young man. He wore faded clothes that were clean and soft with age. I remember that he reminded me wonderfully of the bumbling sweet TV cowboy, Gabby Hayes.

As Uncle Kenny ambled into Barbara and Theresa's house, he announced gruffly to the gang, "Come on, kids, how about a ride in the truck? Okay, then, get ready."

My heart leapt at the prospect.

"Okay, you go ask your mother." Barbara seemed to push me toward home.

"I have to go to the bathroom," Theresa revealed, scurrying into her house.

"I'll be right back! Wait for me!" I bolted across the front lawn of my house, around the red-leafed sticker bushes my mom had planted as a border, and scrambled through the back entrance. "Mom! Uncle Kenny's here! He wants to take us for a ride! Can I go? Please, Mom, can I go?" The words flew from me, breathlessly.

Now, my mother was not an easygoing person and many times found some obscure benefit in not allowing me to share in simple childhood pleasures. She took her time deciding. The dread of missing out on today's fun loomed as she considered the situation. "Okay, go ahead," she said without emotion and continued washing the breakfast dishes.

Without waiting a moment in which Mom might change her mind, I hurried out of our kitchen to return and wait for Uncle Kenny to finish his visit with his sister.

"Okay, everyone into the truck." He let down the old wooden tailgate so we could all pile in. We girls were the little kids that day; Barbara's older brothers, Billy fourteen and Kevin twelve, jumped onto the truck bed as well.

With a pull on the choke and a lift of the clutch, we were headed south toward the bay. Once the small cloud of smoke had dissipated, we breathed in freedom. I knitted my fingers through the wooden side-slats and knelt looking out at my street whizzing by at twenty-five miles per hour. Theresa nudged me, suggesting that I follow her lead and open my mouth toward the wind, a trick that dried out our mouths and caused saliva to gather under our tongues. We found this thrilling.

Three blocks down, the Ford slowed to a halt. Uncle Kenny called out his window to us, "You kids hungry?" I didn't know a time when bay air and adventure didn't make kids hungry, but I didn't want to end the fun by returning home for lunch. "Hang on!" Mysteriously, Uncle Kenny throttled up the rickety vehicle and continued heading south, past Little Beach, then turning north via an alternate route.

Where are we going? I wondered. *I thought we were headed home for lunch.* I was still confused when we pulled up in front of A&A, the tiny, local market on Montauk Highway.

"Okay, Billy and Kev, you go get a loaf of bread. Girls, you go find a jar of mustard. I'll get the bologna." Even as Uncle Kenny revealed his plan, I still didn't understand. *Was he going to take us home and make sandwiches?*

Barbara, Theresa and I stopped by the Limburger cheese on the way to the mustard. This was a grocery store ritual. We held the wax paper packaging to our noses and grimaced at the smell, "Ewww!" and then continued on our mission. The event was exciting and a bit terrifying; I'd never been sent on my own to do such an important family task as picking out food.

"'Got the bread, Uncle Kenny."

"Here's the mustard."

We all met up at the counter with everything we needed for lunch. The checkout girl dragged the wooden frame, drawing our purchases toward her as she plunked numbers into the silver National Cash Register.

In a moment, we were chugging toward the beach, only this time for a picnic. Using the tailgate as a table, without benefit of plates and with only the butcher paper that wrapped the bologna as a tablecloth, Uncle Kenny topped the bread and meat with a wipe of mustard from his pocket knife, finishing the sandwiches and handing them out to us kids.

I remember thinking that I'd never eaten a sandwich that hadn't been cut in half, or without a plate and napkin. It was about the best bologna sandwich I'd ever had, and I didn't even *like* mustard.

Later we played tag on the beach. Then we explored the treasures that had washed ashore that day. We never tired of gently prodding a horseshoe crab with a stick to watch it lift its long, hard tail in self-defense. The boys were big enough to leap from the mainland to the small island inside the beach cove. We girls amused ourselves writing love letters in the sand as Pat Boone intoned in his popular song. Uncle Kenny sat in his truck and just watched us.

We took the long way home, around the loop that followed the bay. It was sad to end one of the greatest days of summer, but it was getting late, and the rule in our neighborhood was that you had to be home by dinnertime—*or else.*

Uncle Kenny left as suddenly as he had arrived. I never knew where he lived or what he did or when he died. I knew only that he turned an ordinary summer day into an adventure I have never forgotten.

LITTLE BEACH

"YOU WANT TO GO KILLIE FISHING?" I asked Theresa. It was shortly after 7:30 a.m. We'd had our breakfasts, washed our faces, brushed our teeth, and were ready to face another sunshiny summer day.

"Yeah, okay. I'll meet you in front as soon as we're ready."

I ran into my house, found Mom in the bathroom scouring the sink and quickly blurted out, "We're going to Little Beach. I'll bring lunch. I'll be home by six o'clock."

Of all the places where my gang and I played, Little Beach was our favorite. Because it was located halfway down our long street and took us only ten minutes to walk the quarter mile, it was available to us in every season. Mostly we went there in the summer. The adults in our lives took no notice of what we did at Little Beach, but we found new adventures each and every day we spent there.

"Don't be late for dinner," Mom called after me, her voice trailing off as I opened the bread box for four slices and smeared Skippy and some Welch's grape jelly over one of them before slapping two together. I cut the sandwich in half, carefully wrapped my lunch in wax paper, slipped it into my spring jacket pocket and tore out of the house to the garage. There I grabbed my quart glass milk bottle, a long string already tied around its neck, and the short, squat coffee can I used for such occasions and into which I stuffed the extra two slices of bread I'd taken. I hurried to the front of the driveway and saw Theresa and Barbara with their equipment and little June following along.

"We have to bring June," Theresa groaned. "Our mother is going grocery shopping and she needs us to take care of her." When their father was on the late shift conducting passengers on the Long Island Railroad, Connie used their car to do her marketing.

"Okay," I said, begrudgingly accepting our fate. June would slow us down and might get tired before we were ready to come home, but we had no choice. Younger kids tagged along sometimes.

We chatted among ourselves while we walked past the houses we knew so well. I observed Mr. Buckley's house with curiosity. He was a strange, tall, rigid man who sometimes walked past my house on his way to A&A market on Montauk Highway. He never spoke to anyone as far as we could tell; he never even looked our way. He would just walk stiffly down the block each evening, reminding me of Frankenstein's monster. I'd had a nightmare about Mr. Buckley once, and from then on he was the "Spooky Man" of the neighborhood as far as we kids were concerned.

My favorite house was a sweet old one with eight ruffle-curtained windows facing the street. There was a huge tree directly in front of the house that was obviously fully grown before the sidewalks were laid years and years ago. The sidewalk split to go around the tree. Whenever we came up to it, we'd divide quickly right or left and take the appropriate route. It was a game we played automatically.

Just past that house, a small woods met a tiny cross-street that abutted Little Beach. Because Little Beach lay on a corner, dirty sand swept along the curve of the two streets and dipped down to the still water that formed a large circular pool. The flow came from a natural canal that was hidden from view by an island in the center of the pool. Our Dr. Samak had warned Mom not to let my sisters and me swim there because the water was polluted and could harbor the polio virus. While Theresa, Barbara, June, and their Mom, Connie, often swam there with no ill-effects, I only remember the one time I persuaded Mom to allow me to join my friends. The stagnant warm water and soft muddy bottom convinced me not to beg Mom's permission to swim there again.

Playing there, wetting only our feet or hands, was always acceptable, and so armed for the day's adventure, we marched down the little side street, passing the sandy beach and beach grass on our right. A small wooden dock sat where the narrow road abruptly turned left at land's end.

There on the little dock we deftly unwound the string from the bottle neck, placed half slices of white bread into the bottles, and filled the bottles with murky canal water. Then, knotting one end of the string to the bottle neck, we'd slowly lower the bottle into the water. Sitting on the sun-warmed dock, we could watch the little killifish swim around the bottle, cautiously entering it to eat the bread. That's when we'd draw in the string and lift the bottle from the water. We placed the captive fish into the coffee can with enough water to allow them to swim around.

Hours passed this way. We picked up rocks that were particularly interesting from the water's edge. Sometimes we'd find one that was an Indian paint pot. These had a rounded hole in one side of the red stone where we could rub our wet finger to create sienna colored "paint." We would amuse ourselves by drawing designs on our legs and arms while waiting for killies to find their way into our milk bottles.

One time we brought a crab net in case we saw any critters clinging to the old post in the canal. Theresa thought it a great idea to catch a duckling that was last in line following its mother to the beach. Terror struck as the mother duck fluffed herself up to double her size and charged toward us. We scattered in various directions screaming, "Let it go! Get it out of the net!" Theresa twisted and turned the net, trying to free the duckling. There was chaos for a few minutes while we danced to escape the mother while Theresa struggled to free the duckling. The instant the duckling was loose, the mother took her brood and waddled off indignantly to resume her trek to the water.

"Don't ever do that again!" Barbara screeched at her sister.

"I didn't know she'd attack. Sorry."

We had resumed the less dangerous hunt, that for little fish, when we heard the old clam boat chugging down the canal. We knew this boat. It would pull up to the dock where we were playing. It was time to wind up the strings and count up the killies in our coffee cans. Who had the biggest, the most, the smallest—these were all points noted before we gently tipped the can into the water releasing our catch. (Once I had brought my killies home, and Mom made me walk the entire distance back to Little Beach, by myself, to release them.)

We stood as the dock wobbled with the pressure of the clam boat's bumping up against it. The old bayman shuffled across the deck to fasten his lines. His face was lined and brown. He wore rubber hip boots. His hands were large and strong and oh, so rough. He did not acknowledge our presence until he entered his little cabin to change into his old brown pants and plaid flannel shirt. We peered into the window.

"Get out of here, you kids!" His voice was coarse and craggy. He waved us away with an unfriendly hand.

We scampered away, taking our equipment with us, all the time mumbling about how mean the old bayman was and how we didn't like him.

But he was a part of our day. We expected him. His appearance and his scolding were as reliable as the sun's setting, and although he seemed cranky to us kids, he was a loner, a bayman who spent his days raking the bay bottom for clams to earn his way in the world.

Tired and ready for our dinner, we slowly made our way down the little road to our street. June looked back over her shoulder to give one last disapproving look at the bayman who was now unloading baskets of clams.

The orange sun told us it was nearing six o'clock, and we would not be late for dinner. We had had another day at Little Beach.

THE TWINS

FOR REASONS I CANNOT REMEMBER, Mom thought it necessary to switch me into another third grade class shortly after the school year had begun. Since Our Lady of Perpetual Help school held half-day session for grades kindergarten through third, I think it was because she had decided to take a job and wanted me in a class with someone whom she could offer early morning car pool assignments in exchange for late morning take-homes when weather was bad. I shall never know for certain.

I remember that my new teacher was, for the first time in my schooling, a lady rather than a nun. Mrs. Whitehead was not only a lady, but a very glamorous one, complete with bleached platinum hair, ruby red lips, and pancake makeup that gave her skin a velvety look. She smelled not of soap and water like the sisters, but of perfume, and when she walked by in the leopard skin slippers she had traded for her spiked heels in the morning, all the children would follow her by scent as well as sight. She was, in our eyes, a modern Miss Crabtree, and we loved her!

During my first day as the new girl in class, I noticed that there was a set of twins seated near me. They were cute little things with curly golden hair, a smattering of freckles, and turned-up noses. They looked amazingly alike and had a popularity that comes with good looks and "twinness." When one of them asked to use the lavatory, I saw that she chose another girl to escort her out of the classroom, down the hall, and to the lavatory. The twin leaned upon the arm of the other girl because she limped badly. She had a large bandage wrapped around one ankle and obviously could not walk on her own.

By eight years of age, everyone in Our Lady of Perpetual Help School had learned that leaving class was a special treat as well as a privilege. Only the best students were chosen to run errands and relay messages. Average students with the gift of cunning learned to sweet-talk teachers into allowing them adventures outside the classroom. Since I was new to the class and teacher, I did not achieve the former status, and by nature I did not possess the latter.

On this, my first day in Mrs. Whitehead's class, however, my Catholic school destiny was set. In the afternoon session Catherine Schiebel, the hobbling twin, asked once again to use the lavatory. She stood and, distinctly as if she had planned it, asked for *me* to be her helper. I was astounded.

I leapt at the opportunity to be of service to my lame classmate and to leave the drudgery of math for a little walk. I was pleased when Catherine chose me to assist on the following day and for the remainder of the time that her sprained ankle was healing. She had chosen me to be her permanent helper.

The surprise honor did not end with Catherine's limp*less* walk. Catherine and her twin, Karen, asked me to come to their house after school the following Friday. I remember being thrilled and nervous to go to a strange house. Until that point, all my friends lived in my neighborhood and had been there forever.

With Mom's permission and arrangements that she'd pick me up at five o'clock, I packed play clothes in a little round carry case and marched off to school with a new adventure in store. During the school day my stomach fluttered a bit. There were moments when I felt the fear of leaving both home and Mom, and I had thoughts of making up some excuse not to actually go home with the Schiebels, but by the end of day I went along with the plan and figured I could make it until five o'clock.

No bus came to pick us up; we *walked* home! A man in what looked like a police uniform stopped traffic as we crossed Wellwood Avenue. How grand it was when shopkeepers waved hello to us when we walked by their stores. It occurred to me that when you live near a village and walk through it frequently, the shop owners know you. This was true for Karen and Catherine. We passed through a wide alleyway between the Historical Society building and Patsy's Bakery and found ourselves on South First Street. We crossed over, walked through a parking lot, and there, not a five-minute walk from town and school, was the Schiebel house. It was tall, dark brown with white trim. There was a front porch and trees and a side yard that went on and on. Even though it was an old house in the first-settled part of Lindenhurst, it was pristine. I thought it majestic.

Mrs. Schiebel, though not slim and pretty, was soft and gentle. She was like one of the moms on *Father Knows Best* or *The Donna Reed Show*; she was kind yet firm, easygoing yet dutiful.

We did homework at the dining room table; there were milk and cookies. We ran across the lawns and swung on the trapeze that was set up in the yard. We laughed and told secrets. We made plans for more visits, were invited to all the parties and dances, and became inseparable. I was often referred to as the "third twin."

For the next five years, Karen and Catherine, Mr. and Mrs. Schiebel, and their big old house balanced my world. With them I was important and respected and popular, and somewhere deep inside me I knew they were right.

GRANDMA'S HOUSE

"YEAH, MA. SO WHAT MAKES YOU THINK SO? Come on, Ma, it isn't like that." Mom stood at the hallway telephone stand, dust rag in hand. "I think it's all in your head. Let's see what happens." She shifted her weight from one foot to the other. "Okay, I gotta go. The kids are waiting for lunch. Yeah. Okay. I'll call you tomorrow. We'll come over to see you this Sunday." Mom sighed as she clicked the receiver down. In an effort to make up for lost cleaning time, she moved quickly through the living room and then her bedroom, spraying Pledge furniture polish and swiftly passing the rag across the piano, the end tables and her dresser. "I just don't know," she mumbled to herself.

It seemed to me that Mom didn't like talking to Grandma on the phone. She didn't much like talking on the phone at all, but she showed no patience with her mother.

I liked Grandma. I liked visiting her in her tall house in Brooklyn. We would drive for a long, long time—past the toll both, past Coney Island where I could see the roller coaster, past the water slapping up on the dock, and finally, finally we would be there. Looking up, I could see Grandma at her upstairs window, peering through the geraniums she'd planted in the curly, dark green iron window cage. Daddy opened the gate because Carole and I were too small to reach the lever. "Grandma! Grandma! We leapt to kiss her hello when she'd only half-opened the door.

"Shush! Donna' make noise. Donna' bother the tenant." Grandma rented out the few downstairs rooms to some phantom man whom we children were constantly being warned not to bother, but whom we never saw.

Quietly trailing behind the hem of Grandma's floral house dress, we climbed the long stairs, pulling ourselves up with the aid of the banister. Mom, holding baby Bridget, and Daddy, lugging the walker and other baby paraphernalia, followed behind.

Wonderful smells wafted from the kitchen at the top of the stairs. When Grandma wasn't cooking something delicious, she placed an orange peel over the pilot light on the stove. The resulting essence gave the whole house a warm fragrance.

The upstairs rooms surrounded a rectangular landing that faced the stairway. To the right of the kitchen was a very large, dual-function room. On the left was a round dining table with, as Mom called them, "claw feet," as well as a large breakfront cabinet. On the right was the living room. We had to be very careful sitting on the burgundy velvet sofa and the royal blue velvet upholstered reading chairs. Grandma usually put coverlets over the furniture before Carole and I arrived. We didn't mind. We sat alone in that living room for long periods of time, staring at the two large paintings that hung over the couch. They portrayed willowy ladies dressed in gauzy floor-length frocks moseying through a garden. They were other-worldly, beautiful, almost fairy-like. I used to daydream about these ladies. Simply seeing them was one of the special features of visiting Grandma. When I was alone, I ran past the living room for fear that I'd look in and the ladies would be moving in the painting, beckoning me to join them.

There was a phonograph player that Grandma played when Carole and I begged hard enough. Winding it up seemed to cause her impatience. She set the arm to the 78 RPM speed, and saxophones, trumpets, and myriad other instruments came alive, calling us to dance.

Past the living room was Grandma's bedroom. Everything in it smelled faintly of a mixture of Arpege and mothballs. Her bed was soft and cozy, although it had metal head and footboards. The room was lined with wardrobes decorated with inlaid wood and dressers topped with marble. Grandma had no closets, but hung her few clothes inside the tall pieces of furniture, which I found fascinating.

The bathroom was at the end of the hallway. There were tiny octagonal white tiles on the floor and a pull-chain for the light. All the fixtures were very large white porcelain. The toilet, too, had a pull chain to flush, the source of endless conjecture on the part of us children.

I remember one very special time when, at my request, Grandma led me down the stairs. Instead of heading out the front door, she and I made a U-turn at the bottom of the steps and followed the dimly-lit forbidden hallway to the back of the house. There she opened a shiny green wooden door that led to a garden. The sun was shaded by a massive arbor from which grapevines hung. We walked along the moss-covered brick path, and at a particular spot between two aqua hydrangeas, Grandma told me, "You can dig here. Don' makka mess." She handed me a teaspoon, and after a moment she returned to her kitchen. Enchanted, I knelt on the damp bricks and spooned out clumps of earth, creating a hill and a hole. I quietly sang songs I'd learned in kindergarten while I felt the dappled light slowly move across my back. I delighted in watching the squirming of a worm I'd unearthed. The smell of the dirt was sweet. I stood, brushed my hands clean, and followed the brick pathway into the sunshine, around the hedged perimeter of the property, where I found a bench in the corner that had been constructed out of tree limbs. I sat for a moment dangling my feet and then wandered back into the shade garden. Beneath Grandma's kitchen window I called up to her, "Grandma, I'm ready to come in now."

"Okay. You waita minute. I come down. Stay there, Grandma," she called. In the manner of many old-world Italian women, she sometimes addressed me as if she were talking to herself. Within minutes Grandma came to fetch me and led me back through the cavernous corridor, up the stairway, down the long hallway to the bathroom where she painstakingly put the rubber stopper into the drain hole, filled the sink with warm water and gently washed my hands between hers with Ivory soap. Then she dried them with a hand towel. Grandma did not hurry things. She was methodical, especially with important affairs like washing my hands.

After a dinner of vegetables, frittata, and macaroni with sauce, we'd all kiss Grandma goodbye. I took a long breath of her before the kiss and hug were over, enough to last me until the next time we visited. We piled into the station wagon and were on our way home. The day had seemed to vanish.

I loved going to Grandma's house.

GRANDMA MOVES IN

THERE HAD BEEN SEVERAL PHONE CALLS NOW. "Okay, Ma. Yeah. Okay, Pat is starting the work this weekend. Get what you can for it."

The bits and pieces of information that I gleaned from these conversations and from those between Mommy and Daddy was that Grandma had been very lonely living in her big Brooklyn house all by herself since Grandpa died. I didn't remember Grandpa, who died when I was just six months old. The plan was that Grandma would sell the house and give Mommy five thousand dollars so Daddy could build an apartment for her in what was the attic of our house.

Daddy took all the Christmas decorations that were stored on the plywood planks he had once laid across the attic beams and moved them into the basement.

Each weekend and in the few hours he had at night after work, Daddy went up to the attic and hammered. "Don't come up here," he'd call to me when I asked if I could help him. "It's dirty and dangerous."

Eventually, Daddy finished his handiwork. He called in Artie Vecio, the next door neighbor and a professional plumber, to connect the kitchen sink and install the bathroom. When it was all completed, Daddy painted the two large rooms and the bathroom and invited the family up to see the apartment. Here Grandma would have a bedroom, a bath and a living room which opened to a small kitchen.

I was excited by all the changes to our house and waited to see what would happen next.

"Stay out of the way today," Mom announced one day at breakfast. "Grandma's moving in today, and there will be a moving truck bringing in her furniture." Mom was jittery; she didn't like messes, and there seemed to be a big one coming today.

A huge truck backed up into our driveway. It was so heavy it cracked the cement in several places. Two men carried in Grandma's table. They had separated the round top from the claw feet. It stood in our kitchen. "Take it if you want it. It's old and dark, and way too big," Mom said to the moving men who then returned Grandma's table to the truck.

"Marion, no!" Grandma cried, her voice high-pitched and torn with the idea of losing so many of her old and familiar things. "Why you wanna give away the table? What am I gonna use?"

"We'll get a new small one, Ma. This one is too big. It's old junk."

Battling the entire time, Mom allowed Grandma to crowd her apartment with a wardrobe made of inlaid wood, the sofa and chairs, a rocking chair, and a corner chair.

"Where are the pictures of the ladies?" They were not in the influx of Grandma's things, and I knew that the sofa and chairs would appear unfinished without them.

"No more junk!" Mom pronounced. "There's too much stuff up there now." With her words, out went crystal, china, gramophone, and countless other treasures. Daddy brought them to the dump, casting them off like so much trash.

Grandma, who loved to sew, was able to convince Mom to allow her treadle Singer sewing machine to be carried up the stairs to her space.

When the day was over, Grandma settled in. She made up her bed with the soft white flannel sheets she'd brought. She laid doilies she'd crocheted years before on top of her furniture. She placed a bit of orange peel on the pilot light. She slept in her new home and prepared for her new life with her daughter, son-in-law, their two little girls, and baby.

It took some time for the rhythm of life to find its tempo with the addition of Grandma. Mom, who liked to do her housework without interruption from her small children, now had her own mother to contend with. "What now, Ma? What do you want now?" She looked up from her vacuum to her mother, who was holding a newspaper.

"Marion, what's thees word? I try to read, but I don' understand thees word."

"'Occupation.' The word is 'occupation.' Now let me get this finished. I have a million things to do." Mom nearly barked her answer.

"Marion, why you talk like that? It's not nice." But Grandma's words were lost in the roar of the vacuum which Mom had restarted, and she retreated to her apartment dejectedly.

Later in the afternoon, Grandma poked her head into our living room where her apartment entrance opened. Mom was taking her afternoon nap on the couch. Grandma tiptoed past Mom to our bedroom where she found Carole and me looking at the pictures in the two books Carole had brought for us from the library. Carole read the words she knew and we improvised the rest. "You wanna milk and a cook? Grandma wanted company.

"Yay, we applauded in a hushed tone.

"Okay, come, I give you."

We sneaked past Mom and quietly climbed the stairs. Grandma gave us each a tiny glass filled with milk and one vanilla cookie.

"This is fun!" Our enthusiasm made Grandma smile, but the delight was broken when Mom called up the stairs.

"What are you two doing up there?"

We looked to each other and then to Grandma. "I just give them a cook and some milk."

"No, Ma! You're gonna ruin their appetites. Do me a favor, huh, and don't take care of my kids!"

Grandma held her tongue and ushered us toward the stairs. Her eyes were dim and stared down at the floor.

I grew to understand that I'd lost Grandma's Brooklyn house forever, that we would never return there. Grandma had lost her independence, but, as she was to learn step by step, Grandma did not, nor would she ever, lose her loneliness.

THE GIRAFFE KNEW

EACH YEAR MOM AND DADDY took Carole, Bridget, Margie and me on day trips. One such adventure was to the Bronx Zoo. I remember being elated with anticipation. What marvels we would see now that the zoo had been renovated, and the animals were no longer confined in small cages. Jungle-like acreage had been created to allow the animals to roam in their natural habitats.

On such trips, I was delegated to vie for the back window seats with Bridget and Margaret. Carole was allowed to sit in the front between Mom and Daddy because she was the oldest. This arrangement never seemed fair to me, since Carole would always be the oldest and had done nothing to earn her status. All the same, I decided not to argue the point today, as it would have made Mom mad and my sisters annoyed at me. I decided to give my two younger sisters the windows seats, and we were off for a day of fun.

Just as the car slowed behind another to enter the park, I pulled myself forward to look out the front window. There I witnessed a horror. A squirrel darted into the street, and the car ahead of ours deliberately ran over it. The creature had not been killed, though; it flailed wildly trying to move out of danger. It seemed to be impaled onto the pavement, some part of its little body frozen into submission by the tire.

Ready to bolt from our vehicle, I said, "Daddy, let's go. Let's help it!" I was stunned when Daddy didn't budge. "There's nothing we can do.

That squirrel is as good as dead," he said, and slowly we passed over the tormented little beast, our tires missing it. I stared at it through the back window feeling helpless and guilty, and I cried with disappointment in my father who, I'd thought until now, could fix anything.

Sadness hovered over me like a pall as my family, and I walked through the park. It seemed nobody cared about what had just happened except me. Mom scowled at me. "Come on. Get over it! You're not going to be sad the entire day, are you? Snap out of it!" That was an order from Mom, and I'd learned years before that one had best not disobey one of Mom's orders.

We found ourselves standing alongside an expanse of land that housed the giraffes. I climbed up onto the first rail of the fence which protected the animals from the humans. There I wondered at their grace and strangeness.

Suddenly one of the giraffes cantered toward us. Many onlookers called to it, coaxing it to come closer. It seemed to set its gaze on me and stopped directly in front of me. I was looking up into its gigantic eyes when, without warning, this amazing animal leaned down and kissed me. Its long dark tongue passed across my face as if I were a lollipop, leaving a stripe of gooey wetness across my tear-stained cheek. Something happened to me in that moment. I knew that this animal was thanking me for my sensitivities toward the little creature I'd like to have saved not long before. It looked deeply at me, then turned around, and ran to its mates.

My parents gazed at me quizzically. My sisters were agog. I stepped down, okay now, feeling calm and connected. "Come on! Let's go look at the zebras!"

TWO DAYS AT THE POVEROMO HOUSE

IT WAS BEAUTIFUL THAT DAY: a sunny, warm, spring Saturday when all the school kids were glad to be free and playing. Mom jingled the car keys in an impatient hand while Carole buttoned her sweater. Carole's short hair flew in different directions as she huffed out of the house. "I'm going to Paula's house," she taunted me. "We're going to play games and eat lunch there."

My heart raced. I wanted to go too. I wanted to spend the day with Paula's younger brother, Glenn, and play games and eat lunch. But Carole had extended no invitation. I was going to be left at home with Mom and the baby again.

Mom ushered the two of us out of the house. "Hurry up," she pushed us along. "I want to get back before the baby wakes up."

The tan station wagon, its side paneled in wood, swished past trees, signs, and the wild tiger lilies that lined Montauk Highway. It turned right at the movie theater, left at the old telephone company, and slowed to a stop. I'd never seen Paula and Glenn's house before. To me it was something out of a vintage film, a big old rambling thing set way back from the street. Trees canopied the lawn throwing dappled light over Mrs. Poveromo as she walked toward the car, drying her hands on a dishtowel. She leaned into the car with a smile. Her blond hair shone in the sun and her eyes glittered hello. The two moms chatted while Carole teetered out to the curb. "Oh, Grace, why don't you join us," Mrs. Poveromo seemed to sing, her voice soft. "Glenn's inside. He'll be happy to see you."

"Well?" Mom raised her eyebrows, pressing me to decide.

How could I go? What would I say? I was torn. Oh, I wanted to jump out of the car and run with my sister and Paula, but I was terrified. Would they like me? I'd miss Mom, all those hours apart. I'd be homesick for sure. Maybe Carole would tell the kids jokes about me, awful things that would make me stumble with my words and be embarrassed. I was seven years old.

I found the words, "No thank you," slipping out of my mouth, though inside I wanted with all my heart to stay. I wanted to laugh and be part of the fun. But terror at being away from my mom and home won the battle, and without discussion or prompting or the slightest care, Mom waved goodbye to Carole and the Poveromos and we drove off.

"I really want to go," I whispered when we'd doubled around the old telephone company.

"Well it's too late. I'm not a taxi service. I'm not driving back."

"Please, Mommy, oh please. I really want to go."

"Too late." Her face smoothed and she smiled.

"Please, Mom," my voice quivered. "I *really* want to go. I'll be good. I thought about it. I really want to go. Oh, please, Mommy, please drive me back."

"It's done," she raised her voice, and we returned home.

My morning was spent in misery. I cried remorseful tears for an hour, and that was enough for Mom. "Now I'll give you something to cry about," she lashed out and headed for the hall closet where Dad's belts hung.

As if in a ritual dance that we both knew so well, I ran crying, "Please Mommy, please no," and plunged onto my bed. Moments later she was on me furiously, raising the belt. It was as if some monster inside her had taken possession of her arm as the belt slammed onto me. Her black eyebrows arched upward, and she breathed hard while lashing me over and over again.

"Now you can cry! Now you have something to cry about! And you'd better not let your father you were so bad that I had to spank you."

In her newfound peace, Mom returned to her housework as I lay on the bed sobbing at the stings on my back and legs.

Later that day, Carole lumbered into the station wagon and waved goodbye to the Poveromos. Mrs. Poveromo smiled at me. "Next time you visit with us too, Grace."

"We had sandwiches and ice cream at lunch and we played games." Carole licked the melting red ice pop she held, tempting me all the way home. "You can't have a taste, either."

Mom reminded her, "Don't drip on the car seats."

I wondered if Mrs. Poveromo had seen my swollen eyes. I hoped not. I liked her, and I wanted her to like me.

The "next time" I'd waited for came two years later with a personal invitation for me to attend Paula's birthday party as Glenn's partner. I was in fourth grade and found the invitation confusing. I showed it to Mom. "It says here to 'come as partner.'"

"No, it's kind of Western. It's 'come on, partner,'" was Mom's explanation, and so she purchased a gift for me to present to Glenn.

I had finally made it to the Poveromo house as an invited guest and was very nervous walking up the long lawn. There, Paula ended the confusion by telling me, "No, it's *my* party. You were invited as Glenn's partner." Everyone laughed as Glenn delightedly opened his gift. I could feel my face flush as I stammered my explanation. I was, as usual for me, left deeply embarrassed.

After the party, Mom picked me up. "Hurry up. Get in. Dinner's on the stove."

"The party was for Paula, not for Glenn," I tried to tell her of the mistake.

"Oh, it doesn't make any difference," she answered flippantly. But it *did* make a difference. I wanted to do the *right* thing, bring the *right* gift, *know* what was going on, and be *sure* of myself.

I realized then that I would find no direction from Mom if I were to be sure of myself. If I were to be accepted, I'd have to look to others, other kids and other mothers, for guidance. I was determined to learn what was deemed appropriate and what was not. In this way, I would not be embarrassed by my ignorance of a social situation. My sensitivity to Mom's moods that I'd developed in order to avoid her wrath, now expanded. Slowly, by inches, others became my models who led me to determine who *I* was, what *I* liked, disliked, and believed.

MY PROMISE

ALTHOUGH LINDENHURST WAS NOT a particularly noteworthy place, I thought it was heaven. It stretched lazily across several miles of the Great South Bay, a perfect place for us kids to find adventure. There were plenty of woods to play in, and few cars interrupted our street games. My neighborhood was made up of rows and rows of identical Cape Cod style houses that had been built for returning WWII soldiers to occupy with the new brides who were waiting for them. My mother was one of those brides. With the move from Brooklyn with a toddler and a six-month-old baby, her dream, printed under her high school yearbook photo, "buying and decorating a house of my own," came true. Little by little, with money pinched from tight budgets, the undistinguished houses took on individuality—this one with a small front porch, that one with a new garage. When I was very little, my mom planted two small weeping willows at the front corners of our hundred-foot lot. By the time I was old enough to go out by myself, the trees towered over me, sweeping across the lawn like two graceful ballerinas. They made my house special and, I thought, very pretty.

The neighborhood children were divided into two groups: the public school crowd, into which my play pals, Theresa and Barbara Bernat next door, fit and the Catholic school group, to which I belonged. The fact that we attended different schools left us with great curiosity about what the others did in school all day. I suppose that they pictured me suffering under the cruel tyranny of the nuns, and I envisioned them in a flurry of flying paper airplanes and chaos. When we arrived home, however, all differences were cast aside, and we were off playing until dinnertime. Except for one particular day.

It seemed like any other weekday as I trudged off the bus at the corner of Deauville Parkway and Maple Street, lugging my heavy brown leather schoolbag. I was in the second grade, and the book load was heavy. The autumn wind gently pushed open the unzipped front of my plaid, lightweight jacket, revealing my dark green uniform. I wanted to get home to take off the jumper, the white blouse, the green knee-high socks, and the brown oxford shoes and get into my dungarees and polo shirt—my play clothes.

As I turned the corner of Maple onto my street, Venetian Boulevard, I felt confused. Something was wrong, but it took me an instant to place it. As I passed the woods where we kids regularly played, I saw my house—without the trees! The weeping willows were gone! The house looked naked and unnatural without them. *What could have become of them? What strange force had come while I was busy at school and swept my beautiful trees away, leaving only two small mounds of sawdust?*

I barreled through the back door. "Mom! Mom! What happened to the trees? They're gone!"

Casually, as if this were a daily occurrence, Mom said, "Yes, I had them cut down. Their roots were wrapping around the water pipes."

"But, Mom, why didn't you tell me? How long had you been planning this? Why didn't you say something?"

"What's to say? I made a decision. Now go get changed and get outside."

The matter was over. I had not been granted a last look, nor said goodbye to the trees that had been part of my childhood. I had never considered they might be obliterated. They had been strong and stationary, solid and permanent, or so I had thought. But even permanent things, I learned, could be removed. I had no say in the matter, and what a child wanted was of no consequence. And so I grew used to the new look of my house, but never again was it as beautiful as it once was.

✂

Pets abounded in my neighborhood. Kittycat was our black and white prince. He slept in the house, sat on one or the other of our laps at television time, and acknowledged us kids as he passed us on his way to his own adventures outside, where he spent his days chasing birds and snoozing under the shrubbery. He was one of the family.

The Bernats had lots of pets. Kevin, Theresa and Barbara's brother, kept pigeons, which bothered Mom passionately when they alighted on our roof and made their mess there. The family had a parakeet which whistled along with Mrs. Bernat, known to me as Connie, while she did her housework. The dogs, Lucky and Candy, played outside with us and roamed freely (which also irked Mom). But the Bernats were unique in that they also had a pet duck—a big white fluffy duck called Jopenna, named, I learned many years later, after a radio performer of the day. Jopenna lived in the yard and took refuge from storm and darkness in the "duck house" Kevin had built for him.

Life with pets was natural for us kids. When I was ten years old, Theresa, a year older, and Barbara, a year younger, and I were expected not only to play with them, but also to feed and groom them, which we did with great reluctance. Chores cut into playtime.

One day Theresa told me that Jopenna was dead—killed by some animal. We all felt distressed and stared at the empty "duck house" and water bowl. Flurries of white feathers clung to the grass around Jopenna's space, evidence of the previous night's treachery. We could only guess what monster had taken away the sweet creature we'd known for years.

That night after dinner, I noticed that Kittycat's bowl was missing. Then I observed that Kittycat was nowhere around.

"Mom, where's Kittycat?"

Mom was stirring a pot that simmered on the stove. "He killed Jopenna next door. I had your father take him to where he was working today and drop him off. He's gone."

"What! Kittycat didn't kill Jopenna! He wouldn't do that!" I yelled.

"Connie told me that something killed Jopenna. It had to be Kittycat. Now he's gone. That's enough about it," she added casually.

"No!" I faced her squarely. "No, it's not enough about it! You had no right! How could you? Where is Daddy working? I want him to bring Kittycat back!"

"Don't raise your voice to me, young lady." But I didn't care that Mom was angry. My rage overcame my fear of her.

"You do whatever you want. You don't care about anyone or anything but yourself! That little Kittycat didn't do anything to hurt anyone— ever—and now you've thrown him away! I want him back, do you hear? I want him back!" My screams turned into sobs. "When I have children, I'm going to ask them about things. I'm going to find out what they think before I make big decisions. I'm never going to be like you! I'm going to ask them!"

"Oh, no you won't," Mom said. "You'll see. When you have children you'll do the same as me. Now go inside, and wash your face."

The argument was over. Mom had won. There was nothing left for me to do.

When Daddy came home from work, I jumped at him. "Where's Kittycat? Where did you leave him? Can you get him back, Daddy?"

Daddy looked at Mom then at me. "I left him in Patchogue. It's twenty miles away."

"How could you, Daddy? How could you?" I yelled, agony returning to my voice.

"You can't have an animal that kills other animals. We had to get rid of the cat," was all he could give me in the way of an explanation.

"Don't upset your father," Mom said. "Get ready for dinner, and that's the end of it!"

I didn't speak to my parents for two days. Mom came in from the garage where she'd put out the trash into one of three large garbage pails there. "Well what do you know? There's an opossum sleeping in the pail. There are a few duck feathers too. Well, what do you know?"

Kittycat returned home a week later. He had been pretty well beaten up and starved by the journey. I fed him and held him and spoke love words to him while I caressed him. He'd walked the twenty miles home. How he found us I could never figure out. He was just that kind of cat— smart and brave and true. No one brought him to a vet; Mom said we couldn't afford it. The infection in one of his wounds got the better of him, and he died a few days later.

Mom continued to make all the decisions for everyone. I vowed that I would never, never be like her.

Years later I gave birth to my only child, my daughter, Stephanie. I called her "my experiment" and promised to bring her up in the way I wish I had been raised. I would ask her what she thought before making family decisions, even little ones. The consideration, the sense of self, the value I gave to my daughter not only proved me right, but also allowed me to experience the adventure of growing up all over again, happily, with her.

MY DAD

MY DAD WAS A VERY SPECIAL PERSON. Wherever he entered a room, he made everyone there feel important. I don't remember him ever saying a bad word about anyone or doing anything mean. When he came home from work, he loved to sit down at the head of the dinner table and be with his family. After dinner he'd sit in his favorite upholstered chair in the living room to read. He was the one who read stories to my sisters and me when we were little. He paid attention to me. I loved my dad.

Dad was good with tools and could build anything. I don't know how or where he learned his skills, but he let me help him when I was quite small, and so I learned how to use tools. When I asked my neighbor's father, a professional electrician, to direct me as I changed a lighting fixture on the front porch of my house (I have a healthy respect for electricity and didn't want any shocking surprises), he said amazedly, "You handle tools like a man." I proudly accepted the compliment.

After Dad's many years as a house painter resulted in several slipped discs in his back and bursitis in his shoulders, he was able to establish a position at the race track. He loved his new job. Managing the bay of five-dollar windows at the race track afforded him time to play golf each weekday morning before opening the window for the New York Racing Association at ten in the morning. He found the races exciting, the horses exquisite, and the owners and jockeys interesting. When school began and all his daughters needed new shoes, Daddy would earn extra money doing paint jobs on the weekends for people he knew.

At home Daddy was pretty quiet, leaving Mom to run the household and raise us kids. As little children, we learned not to bother our father and not to jump on him in play. He loved my mother very much and she was crazy about him. When Daddy was home, all was quiet and peaceful.

There were many times I realized that Daddy favored me. He'd whisper to me when we were alone, "Grace, you're the smart one." Often he would tell me stories that he didn't share with anyone else. He told me about the time he was hospitalized in England for a bullet wound suffered during the war and the nurse he met there. He told me of his little sister, Mary, whom he loved very much. As was the custom in Italy when he was a boy, an older child would take responsibility for a younger. Daddy had been appointed Mary's guardian. When she was two and Dad was about eight years old, they and their older bother came down with typhoid fever. Daddy recovered but Mary and their brother did not. Daddy never spoke of Mary again until he was on his deathbed.

When Daddy began working at the race track, he asked me to go shopping with him for new sports jackets and ties. It was a lovely spring evening when he drove us to Martins, an upscale clothing store nearby. I picked out a darkish, burnt orange jacket, a blue jacket, and ties to match each. I even chose some light blue shirts, upgrading Daddy's style from his usual white. We laughed and had fun together. When we arrived home, Mom didn't say much, so Daddy quietly put his new clothes away. But the next day when he came home after work, my sisters and I made quite a big fuss over his new look while Mom busied herself with dinner preparations. He was so happy.

While we were all sitting at the table, I said, "Daddy, we have to complete your new look." With that I fetched a comb and some hair pins. I combed his straight-back, beautiful golden, wavy hair to the side and pinned it down. I spritzed a little of Mom's hair spray and then removed the hair pins. The new look was set and Daddy looked ten years younger. The following weekend, Uncle Dom and Uncle Sam visited with their wives and all admired Daddy's new look. They went home and changed their hair styles as well.

When I was home from college one spring break, Mom wanted a border placed in front of our house between the lawn and the street. Daddy bought railroad ties and one Saturday morning began to dig out the spaces. I arrived at the house as he was starting the project. I went into the garage, grabbed another shovel and began to dig with him. Neither of us spoke. He acted as if we were old working buddies which, I suppose, we were. When we took a rest I was amazed when he said, "Drace (his nickname for me), go get two beers." We sat on our stoop admiring our handiwork and sipping together. After we finished the job, we were tied together in a secret bond as adults. The railroad ties remain today, decades later.

There were unspoken rules in our house. I was deeply hurt when my high school friend left our house one Saturday. Daddy had remarked, "That Betty is a pretty cute girl." Daddy had never said that I was cute or pretty or anything more than "okay" when I asked how I looked. How I longed for him to see me and think I was pretty. I suspect he avoided crossing Mom by not complimenting me.

Aunt Rose and Uncle Mike celebrated their twenty-fifth wedding anniversary with a huge party in a catering hall. It was the closest thing to a wedding we'd seen in a while. Daddy danced with many of my cousins, but he didn't dance with me. I never said anything to him, for I got the feeling that he felt it better not to.

Years later, I drove to Brooklyn to take my Aunt Alice to lunch. She was not actually my "aunt" but my mother's best girlhood friend and my godmother. She explained to me that when I was born, my father had proclaimed, "This one is mine." After that, Mom refused to hold me except for quick feedings, and she told others, including Aunt Alice, not to hold me, to leave me in the baby seat, because Mom was afraid of my getting sick. It seems that even as a baby, I was subject to constant manipulation by a woman who simply did not like me and wanted to hold me back from fun, from love, from joy.

Without anyone actually declaring it, my mother and I were opponents. When things went wrong, she usually found a way to make it my fault. When I wanted something, she'd declare that it was not a good thing to have. Mom's first child, Carole, was her favorite; I was Dad's. Thankfully, my dad believed in me and kept my spirits up while maintaining peace in the home. It was he who made me smile and coaxed Mom into letting me take my first job in high school. It was he who encouraged me to continue college when I wanted to quit. When my dad was around, life was good. Unfortunately, like many men of that time, he just wasn't around very much. I think of my dad often and the lessons he taught me about life and people continue to guide me. I wish I could have had him with me longer, but that was not to be.

THE *SEA BEE*

ALTHOUGH HE HAD HAD NO experience in boating, when I was seven years old, Daddy purchased a 32-foot fishing boat for the family and handled it as if he were born to the sea. I don't know if there had been any conference about this transaction with Mom. It seems that one day Daddy drove the family to a dock, pointed to a long teak-clad vessel and asked, "How do you like her?" My sisters and I were awestruck. Mom was thrilled at the prospect of spending time as a family out on the Great South Bay, and it was her intention to do just that at every available moment. Although Daddy wanted to name our boat "Cargrabrimar" after us kids—Carole, Grace, Bridget and Margaret—it seemed the paperwork and expense prevented that horror from becoming a reality. Our boat remained the *Sea Bee* which sounded fine to me.

Each Saturday and Sunday we packed up the fishing gear and the lunches Mom had prepared the night before and donned heavy sweatshirts. We all loaded into the station wagon and headed for Ruthrig's Marina where we quickly and efficiently loaded the *Sea Bee*.

"Okay!" Dad called. "Let her go!" and I released the lines to the bow while Mom took care of the stern lines. Carole found her favorite spot on the bow deck where she stretched out to nap. Bridget and Margie were small and stayed near Mom. We chugged out of the canal slowly, strictly obeying the "No Wake" signs.

I sat on the bow watching a day being born. There were no

voices—only the drone of the *Sea Bee's* engine and the splash of cut water on the dark bay.

Daddy pointed us due south for about a half mile until we reached Fox Island. It was barely an island at all—more like a few acres of mud and grass that had the privilege of being higher than its surroundings. Here a wooden dock hung loosely together around gas pumps.

"Ready? Okay, tie her up!" Daddy called to me, and I hooked our line around one of the stanchions that moaned as we sidled up to it. He ran to the stern to tie the other line. With deep concentration and the deft motions of a musician, Mom continued rigging the fishing poles for whatever might be running that day. The sudden silence stirred Carole awake. She languidly turned her head to look at the scene and silently dismissed the rest of us to resume napping.

"Can I look for crabs, Mom?"

"Me too! Me too!" Bridget, though only four, loved adventure.

"Take your sister and watch her," Mom ordered me while lifting the little one onto the dock then handing me the crab net.

"Okay, Bridget, hold on to my shirt and don't get too close to the edge," I warned, gingerly moving along the dock, peering over the side.

It is with a trained eye that one distinguishes a blue claw crab from the green-weedy side of the dock to which it clings. I possessed such an eye. "I see one!" I called toward the boat. Slowly at first, then with a swift scooping motion, I swished the net onto the side of the dock and came up with a big one.

"Bring it over!" Mom raised the wooden bushel basket for my catch. "Good size," she approved and continued her rigging.

Having completed my inspection of the dock, I handed Mom the net, took Bridget by the hand and walked up the inclined path toward the bait shack. "Be careful of the loose boards, Bridg," I cautioned my little sister as we went to meet Daddy.

The familiar smell of mildew mixed with that of fish and salt water hit us when we opened the door. Thousands of fishing hooks and lures decorated the walls. The aisle in front of the counter was lined with galvanized buckets, wooden killie traps, twine, and buoys. We were at home here. We knew this place; we were bay children.

Daddy paid for gas, and we were off toward adventure!

Some days we'd go to Garbage Cove to crab with killie rings. Other days, when fluke or flounder were running, we'd head toward Captree Bridge, where Daddy would give me the signal to toss anchor off the bow, then reverse the engine until the anchor grabbed the bottom. We drew a large depth of water and so had always to be careful not to run aground.

As the day brightened, we slowly peeled away layers of clothing, first sweatshirt, then long-sleeve polo shirts, until we were down to our bathing suits. On very warm days Daddy brought us off the channel to a spot where other boats were not likely to pass. There he would anchor and roll the wood-and-rope ladder off the side. "Hop in!" he'd say, and before he finished speaking, we'd be off the boat into the water splashing and swimming. Bridget wore a life jacket until she was older. Baby Margie stayed with Mom.

Salty and sunned, we gathered on the fishing deck while Mom handed out sandwiches. "Bologna with mustard."

"Me, me," cried Bridget.

"Ham and Swiss with mayo."

"That's for me!" I loved ham and Swiss, especially with mayo.

We were never so hungry nor did food ever taste quite as good as when we ate on deck.

There were rare times when Mom invited others to join us. Mostly it was Aunt Toni, Uncle Dom and Clara, because they'd arrive early enough that we could set out at out at dawn as usual. It was on one such day at noonish that we found ourselves anchored. The adults were fishing, Daddy was below using the head and Carole was napping. I was chatting with my favorite cousin, Clara, when I looked over the side and caught sight of the top of Bridget's head with her hair suspended and streaming all around it.

"Bridget fell in!" I shouted, and in a moment Mom jumped overboard to lift her four-year-old out of the water. Aunt Toni and Uncle Dom reached down while Mom repeated, "Get the baby. Take the baby first."

Bridget was unharmed, though Mom's saddle shoes squished when she was hauled back onto the deck. Without thinking Mom said, "Okay, everything's fine." She stripped off the wet clothes down to her bathing suit, pushed the hair out of Bridget's eyes, dried the two of them off with a towel and resumed fishing. "Just leave her alone, and she'll forget all about it." That was that.

Daddy emerged. "What's all the commotion?" He paled when we told him about what he'd missed. "I thought all the ruckus was because the crab basket spilled over."

There was no discussion. There was no hugging. The only noticeable change was that the following week we discovered that Daddy had put child safety fences along both sides of the deck.

We were bay children. We knew the sky and the tides. We could cut a bloodsucking worm with a knife as it squirmed and thread it to a hook. Whatever explanations or understanding we sought, we took from the golden reflections of sunset as we headed home, the red light blinking off the starboard side. We were salty and tired and would sleep well that night.

BY EXAMPLE

I LOVED GOING TO GRAMMAR SCHOOL. Yes, we had horror stories to tell. There were nuns and lay teachers alike whom we found loud, mean, and objectionable in a variety of ways. We still tell the stories of cruelty and injustice these many years later. But the key here is that *we* tell the stories. *We* were in it together. "*We*" were the students in my class. From third grade, when Mom had me transferred from Sister Mary Christopher's class to Mrs. Whitehouse's, I spent close to eight hours a day, five days a week, ten months a year for six years with the same forty youngsters. *We* were a family of sorts. We knew each others' habits, laughed at each others' goofy mistakes, accepted each others' inadequacies and basically got along together. I don't remember there ever being a fight between any of my classmates. A common enemy was there in the room with us, so we bonded together to survive. Except for Mrs. Whitehead, I don't remember a gentle teacher or a loving nun in the entire school.

We'd established a pecking order early on, and I lucked out. Since I was bright, the teachers generally accepted me, and because I was fun to be with, the kids liked me. I was in with the "in" crowd and comfortable, albeit not perfectly safe, in Our Lady of Perpetual Help's class, my home away from home. Except for the infrequent occasions when Sister would be exceptionally out of sorts and cruel, the rules of survival were clear and easy to follow: be neat, be prompt, be mannerly, be smart, be prepared, and beware. Coming from my particular home environment, I was quite familiar with the situation and able to glide through my days relatively unscathed. Other children were not as fortunate.

In fourth grade our class was housed in the Annex building located north of the school, past the church. One day the quiet, reserved Ralph Bertham asked, in his gentle British accent, to be excused to the boy's room. Sister Angel denied the request, not just once but three times. Poor Ralph, like the rest of us, never dreamed of simply getting up and leaving the room without permission, and so he sat until finally he wet his pants.

We were appalled to witness Ralph's humiliation, and to make matters worse, Sister Angel was actually angry with him. She had Ralph report to the office way over in the main building, wet pants and all. He never returned. I think his parents placed him in public school, or maybe the family moved. All I know is that Ralph was suddenly gone, and life in school resumed what passed for normalcy. We learned to hold it in. We learned by example.

Part of that normalcy was our being allowed to perform in front of the class each day after lunch. A typical act was Glenn Poveromo's animated pretend band. Glenn "pretend played" lead guitar while Matty Shore and Eddy Flynn "pretend played" bass and backup guitars while a recording of the actual song wailed out. All three sang and gyrated. The most famous of their numbers was *Stagger Lee*, followed closely by *All American Boy*. Oh, how we all laughed and applauded! The work of the day was almost forgotten by the time Sister Angel returned to the front of the room with her multiplication wheel. (It seems that, in all the joy of third grade, Mrs. Whitehead had never sufficiently taught us our times tables. Sister Angel remedied the unacceptable situation, accompanied by sneers for our former teacher.)

In fifth grade we learned the art of "tuning out." Mrs. Brown never spoke. Instead this stumpy, unattractive middle-aged woman shouted. She shouted roll call. She shouted directions. Mostly, though, she shouted scoldings. There were times my ears rang from all her shouting.

In Mrs. Brown's class our primary source of knowledge was derived from coloring. We colored in maps for geography, historical scenes for history, diagrams for English, and fractional pieces of the pie for arithmetic. Because we were older, we colored with Venus Paradise pencils rather than crayons, and as we filled in countries and presidents and phrases and blueberry pies, Mrs. Brown would holler. Even this became home.

I think the vast collection of colorful lessons overwhelmed Angela Funi. Angela was not organized. Nor was she neat. Angela was our class "Pigpen" and we accepted her for that. But Mrs. Brown found her fodder for a booming rant one day when papers wafted out of Angela's desk onto the floor. Poor Angela was struggling to find her homework. The more passionately Angela rifled through her desk, the louder grew Mrs. Brown until, red-faced and out of control, our teacher tipped the desk over, spilling myriad papers, half-eaten apples and used tissues onto the floor.

"Stand up!" she commanded.

Angela stumbled out of her seat.

"What is that on your uniform?" Mrs. Brown pointed to a stain near the OLPH emblem covering Angela's trembling heart.

"It's white clam sauce from yesterday's lunch, Mrs. Brown," Angela whispered.

We were all encouraged to laugh at this comic relief.

After a litany of degrading remarks, Mrs. Brown rolled her eyes. "Now pick up this mess, young lady, and put all those papers in order! What else is in that desk? A rat? I'd hate to see your house if this is how you keep your desk!"

Angela scrambled to pick up the mess but clumsily scattered the papers even farther across the aisle. We could see how impossible her situation had become. There was no way out for her. When our lessons resumed, we all made sure that neatness prevailed. We learned by example.

When Angela went home for lunch that day, she did not return. Shortly thereafter, Angela disappeared from our class.

Sister Ellen, our sixth grade teacher, was a strange combination of positive and negative energies. She had the monumental task of teaching us algebra, clauses, and critical thinking. While she drilled us daily with practice upon practice until we learned each lesson, it was not uncommon for her to swing at—and strike—a student. She was physical, and her words were frequently caustic. But there was also fun in Sister Ellen, and we liked her.

After school, many days I would remain with a few others—not to spend more time with our teacher, but to spend a few moments with Mr. Schmeal, the custodian. Charlie, as we called him, was very old, and he moved slowly. His trousers seemed to float over his bony frame. He had sparse white hair which he parted neatly on the right, and his face, though greatly wrinkled, glowed with rosy cheeks. He spoke to us in dulcet tones, and since we'd helped him move the desks so that he could sweep, he had time to demonstrate his penmanship on the blackboard. Having been schooled in the late 1800s, Charlie's letters were precise and slanted and swirled elegantly at the tops and bottoms. His script reminded me of the copy of the Declaration of Independence Sister had once shown us. He let me practice my letters on the blackboard before he washed it clean for the following day. I learned to write fancy letters, and to be gentle and giving. I learned by example.

Seventh grade was the first time in years that our class was literally elevated out of the basement rooms. Here on the second floor, we were under the tutelage of Sister Susan, a round nun who burped throughout our afternoon classes after her lunch in the convent. Sister Susan was direct. She openly favored Karen and Catherine, the blond, curly-haired twins. She openly disfavored Glenn. He still talks of the day Sister walked him into the boy's room and wet down his hair so it lay flat to his head. He had to wear his hair this way throughout the day. It seems she did not approve of his pompadour, nor did she think he would ever reach his goal, to be an elementary school teacher. In his rage, Glenn thought, *Oh, I will be a teacher, and I will be better than you. I'll be kind.* Glenn learned by example.

By eighth grade our class stood together. We had survived the grades, and if a teacher were unfair to one of us, we all rebelled with looks of disdain and overt silence. By some strange hand of fate, we were assigned Sister Angel a second time. But something had happened to her. Her face appeared thinner, her walk more rigid. The joy she had occasionally afforded us in the fourth grade was gone. She looked at us with an accusing eye when no crime had even been contemplated, let alone acted upon. We had to be especially on our guard.

The parties we'd held at our homes since fourth grade were still our time to socialize without the sisters' surveillance. We still danced, but progressed from the polka and Lindy to the Slop and slow dancing. There were always popcorn and pretzels, cake and soda. Glenn and the boys still performed for us, and sometimes we played spin the bottle. I think Sister suspected more improper behavior simply because we were thirteen years old.

One day as we were working quietly, Sister rose from her desk and walked around the room, up and down the aisles, her hands beneath the front piece of her habit. This was not uncommon. This day, though, as she came up behind Bobby Foy, she reached for his pompadour with her left hand and swooped down with a pair of scissors in her right. By the time we knew what was happening, she'd shorn Bobby's in-style pompadour, asserting, "I told you to get rid of that!" and marched triumphantly out the door.

There was a collective gasp in the room; we were shocked by the quiet violence we'd witnessed.

Bobby yelled, "What'd you do that for?"

As Sister made her exit, the entire class, girls as well as boys, raised their fingers in a defiant obscene gesture—even the quiet Janis Donnel! I had never seen any of my classmates gesture or speak a foul word before. I felt like running out, screaming. I had visions of prison movies flashing through my brain.

Bobby remained in class until the end of the year, but most of us did not speak to Sister Angel again, unless she spoke to us first. Sister had taught us about Gandhi. We learned the power of passive resistance. We learned by example.

OLPH, known to us as Old Ladies Poor House, was a unique adventure. There I learned to trust my friends and mistrust the sisters. I learned to be kind to the weak, help those who needed a hand and accept my peers without judgment. I learned my studies well, and those studies and lessons have served me equally well. With all the good and bad, joys and sorrows, laughter and tears, I learned to be an exceptional teacher. I learned by example.

LOLLIPOPS
AND ROSES

WE WERE ALL SO EXCITED! This was it! We were about to graduate from Our Lady of Perpetual Help Catholic School where we had learned far more than arithmetic and reading. We knew how to be loyal to a friend by remaining silent and taking a rap on the hands, to respect elders and authority by automatically standing when a grown-up entered the room, and to remain self-composed—to a point. That demure, careful attitude—sitting still with hands folded for hours—was quickly forgotten as we prepared for our eighth-grade prom.

For weeks, and to Sister Angel's dismay, all we girls could talk about at recess was what color, style, and fabric comprised our first fancy, grown-up dress. We sat at our desks, all forty of them, which had been arranged row after row in the school's former library.

"I'm wearing a corsage. My mom is buying one for me," Jean Banning chirped.

"I've got clip-on earrings to match my necklace." Kathleen Morris reached across her neck to her ears as if already wearing her new baubles.

"I'm wearing white. And blue. I love my dress." I shared the news while eating my tuna sandwich. It was Friday, June 23rd, 1962, and soon we would be released from our classroom to prepare for the evening we'd all been waiting for!

It seemed that the old school bus took forever to make its way through Lindenhurst. It plodded from one stop to another and finally arrived at mine: Deauville and Maple. I raced home and into the house. I wanted to get everything ready before Mom came in. She'd certainly find some chores for me that would cut short my preparation time.

I was right. "Grace, empty the groceries out of the car," she called as she walked into the house toward her bedroom to change out of her work clothes.

"Okay, Mom!" Best stay on her good side today. I wanted nothing to go wrong. "Anything else you need done?" I tried to stay ahead of her so that the time after dinner would be my own.

"Nothing right now." Not the best answer, but good enough. I could begin. I appraised my appearance and decided to give my hair a quick set. Surely two hours in the pink bobbin curlers would give it a little wave. That done, I filed my stubby fingernails smooth and gently stroked on a single coat of white nail polish. (Blue would definitely have been too bold.) Impatiently waiting for them to dry, I paced around my room blowing at my fingertips. *Oh no, Carole's home. Just remain calm. Don't listen to her.*

"What are you doing?" she asked, looking me over suspiciously.

"Nothing. I just polished my nails."

"Is that my polish? Give it back. Who said you could use my polish?" She reached for the bottle.

"It's mine. I bought it yesterday. Yours is still on the dresser. Look."

"Oh. Okay." She seemed almost disappointed that I had not trespassed onto her side of the dresser.

Problem averted, I headed downstairs for dinner. "Mom, can I eat now? I have to get ready."

"Oh, that's right. Tonight is your little dance. I don't understand why you can't eat with the family and then go."

"Mom, the prom starts at 7:00. Dad won't get home until then. If I wait dinner for him, I'll be late. I have to eat now. Remember, we talked about this already."

"Okay," she reluctantly relented, and I quietly ate some of the previous night's leftovers.

By this time, it was 6:15. I returned to my room to slowly and methodically dress. Garter belt and stockings, slip, and the elegant, delicate, absolutely beautiful white voile dress Mom and I had picked out. It had cap sleeves, a sash at the waist and a bell-shaped hem that came just below my knees. I slipped on the white Queen Ann heels and then took the small blue beaded bag Mom had picked out, the white wool wrap, and the precious bluestone necklace down to the kitchen. "Mom, will you help me with the necklace?" I handed her the strand and she fastened it around my neck.

"I was right. That necklace and purse make the outfit," was her comment.

"Well, how do I look?"

"You look alright. Now let's get you there before your father comes home and has to wait for his dinner."

"But I wanted to show Daddy how I look before I left."

"No time. Let's go."

And like Cinderella, I found myself at the Knights of Columbus Hall with all my friends—the four eighth-grade classes, all together, looking beautiful and handsome.

"Have a good time!" the other parents called as they smiled at us.

"You're getting a ride home with Mrs. Store, right?" Mom asked.

"Yes, Mr. and Mrs. Store are taking us out for pizza afterward. Remember, I already asked you."

"Yeah, okay." And Mom drove away.

We entered the dimly-lit room which seemed to be illuminated only by stars. Each girl was handed a little satin-bound book with a miniature pencil attached by a tiny string. I learned it was called a dance card. I didn't want to write in mine; it was too pretty to use. Music played from a record player, and before I could take off my wrap, Glenn asked me to dance. We did a Lindy, and then Matty asked me for the next one.

We girls giggled at the hors d'oeuvre bar and admired each other's dresses. After seeing one another grow up in green wool jumpers, white blouses, green knee socks, and brown shoes, we were dazzled by the chiffon and lace, pink and white and blue and yellow.

Gerri and Christopher Schneer's older brother, Kenny, a high school senior and one of the K of C's young men who helped organize the dance, called out that we should partner up for the promenade to see who would be king and queen of the prom. No one even knew that such an event was scheduled.

Michael Howard looked at me and gallantly asked, "Shall we?"

"Sure." And with that, we strolled around the room with our classmates to Jack Jones' popular song, "Lollipops and Roses."

As we walked, the high school seniors murmured among themselves. At the end of the song they created a drum roll. "Ladies and gentlemen, we are proud to present to you the king and queen of the prom!" Kenny came up to Michael and me and led us to the stage.

Numbness took over my smile, and disbelief captured me! A young man placed a little tiara on my head and a bouquet of lollipops and roses into my arms. Michael and I were presented with silver identification bracelets, very popular at the time. We sauntered around the room for everyone to gaze upon. This was the first time that I had ever been the center of positive attention and the recipient of admiration.

I spent the remainder of the evening on wings floating in the euphoria of having been singled out and praised.

At 11:00 I quietly entered my parents' bedroom.

"You home?" Mom muttered sleepily.

"Yes," I whispered. "Guess what? I was picked queen of the prom."

"That's nice. Go to bed."

For reasons I could not discern at the time, I stood there and began to cry.

"Why are you crying?" Daddy asked.

"I don't know. I guess I have nothing to look forward to anymore."

"Don't be silly. You have your whole life ahead of you. Kiss your mother good night and go to bed."

The next morning at breakfast Mom placed a column she had cut out of Newsday newspaper in front of me. It reported the events of the previous night—that I had been crowned queen. The event was never mentioned again in our house.

Now, many, many years later, whenever I hear that song, and I do hear it occasionally on the radio stations I favor, I claim it as my own, for I was queen of the prom and of "Lollipops and Roses."

PUBLIC SCHOOL

BECAUSE MY OLDER SISTER, Carole, attended Seton Hall High School in Patchogue, I was expected to follow in her footsteps. No one had ever suggested otherwise to me, and so I joined the best of the OLPH graduates as we took and passed the diocesan entrance exams to attend Catholic high school. I had no idea what to expect. I was fitted for the plaid skirt uniform, and Mom decided that I could use the white blouses I'd worn as part of my elementary school uniform.

On the first day of high school I was jolted out of sleep at 5 a.m. I seemed to wander in a sleepy stupor trying to focus on washing up and dressing. This was definitely not fun! At dawn Carole and I hiked up the two blocks to catch the bus on Montauk Highway. Carole sat with her friends, and I sat alone from Lindenhurst to Babylon when another freshman joined me. I remember being mesmerized each day by a West Islip pickup who always took the front seat with her head covered in curlers. She'd unwrap each curl and tease it mercilessly until her hair extended beyond the size of a beach ball. By the time the bus lumbered into the Patchogue parking lot forty-five minutes later, she had smoothed the surface hairs over the back-combed locks, achieving the perfect style of the '60s, a bouffant coiffure. I thought she looked lovely!

The only time our freshmen group changed classes was to travel to the home economics room where we were taught to sew. (The lay teacher was a sweet woman whose breath reeked of stale cigarettes and coffee. I held my breath when she leaned over to advise me about my sewing.) We also moved to the common room where Mr. Rock taught us ballroom dancing. All the boys stood on one side of the room and the girls on the other. At Mr. Rock's command, the boys stampeded toward us and asked us individually to dance: one step, side, close. Happily, no one was ever injured. Although I enjoyed the dance break, I did not at all like the academic classes. The English teacher, Mrs. Spinley, focused on vocabulary and spelling. There was no discussion of literature. Sister Mary, the biology teacher, was pitiless in her punishments: "Class you'll now copy over today's entire chapter because you did not know it well." I found myself still awake at 11 p.m. finishing homework and then up in the dark of early morning in order to catch the bus.

On weekends I saw my OLPH friends who had gone to Lindenhurst Junior High School. We were still close, but they had new and different interests all geared to public school, which was a mystery to me. I saw Mary Waltz one day. She had been slated to attend Seton Hall with me, but wound up in Lindenhurst Junior High's 9th grade instead. When I asked her what had happened, she just said, "I didn't want to go to Catholic school anymore, so I changed my mind."

It was then that I changed my own mind! I no longer wanted to be a part of Seton Hall, but to attend public school. I was ready to take the plunge into the unknown! I had never even thought about it before, but now I was certain! When I brought this up with my parents, I received an immediate and definite answer—*No!* Each day thereafter when I returned from school, I told Mom how I despised the ride, the school, the people. She and Daddy became angry, but I was used to that. I insisted. I talked and talked about public school at every opportunity. I yelled and stomped and tormented the household until finally in November, Mom said, "Fine. You want to go to public school? Go! But you're not getting any clothes to wear. You can wear your uniform!" *(Right. I'd wear a uniform and be ostracized for life.)*

Hooray! I'd won. Now I had to be quick and clever. I took my babysitting money and walked to the nearby Abraham & Strauss department store where I hunted through the racks for something versatile, inexpensive, and of high enough quality to last. I found a red and cream wool jumper, and a cream turtleneck. Shopping bag in hand,

I marched toward Martins, stopping in the Thom McAn store where I bought a pair of soft red leather shoes to match the jumper. I could alternate them with the black shoes in my closet. In exclusive Martins I found a camel-colored skirt and a black and white herringbone one on the sale rack. Both were wool and fully lined. I matched them with a black sweater and a white blouse. With these items and the one skirt in my closet, I could create enough outfits to wear over the course of several weeks. Each Saturday night I could count on making five dollars babysitting, and that would buy yet another item for my new wardrobe. I was cute and snappy.

I entered Lindenhurst Junior High School privately terrified. Mom had signed me in and walked out without a word. I acted as if I hadn't noticed. Mr. Paperel, my guidance counselor, set up a schedule for me and gave me a map of the building. When I entered Miss Cutie's homeroom, the "W" homeroom, I was approached by a large, tough-looking girl with long night-black hair, black blouse, black tight skirt, and black stockings. I feared that Mom's warnings of juvenile delinquents beating me up were about to come true. "Hey, girly, you a new girl?" She flipped the casual words at me as she stared me up and down.

"Yes," I answered straightforwardly, hiding my fear. I glanced at my red shoes and looked back at her.

"Oh," she said and shuffled away.

She turned out to be like everyone else I met in my new school—friendly, helpful and just another kid.

Eventually I acclimatized to my new situation. Miss Burke, the gym teacher, allowed me to take a white gym suit out of the lost and found box so I didn't have to wear the hideous aqua green one from Seton Hall. Mr. Sandbourne, the science teacher, sat me next to Betty Gomez, who was to become my best friend through junior and senior high school. I joined the chorus and later became involved in school government. Daddy didn't talk to me for six months but finally relented. Mom had never really talked to me, and I was used to her being angry for no apparent reason. I kept to myself at home and hoped that the tension would soon wear off, which it did.

Three years later, seeing that I hadn't turned into a juvenile delinquent and had in fact become quite an active and successful high school student, Mom and Dad asked Bridget if she would prefer Seton Hall or Lindy, as Lindenhurst High School was nicknamed. She chose public school without a second thought and without having to fight for it. Mom took Bridget out to buy a few outfits for her new school days. That same year, my parents plucked Margie, the youngest of my sisters, out of OLPH's sixth grade and flung her into public elementary school, for which she was completely unprepared emotionally, but for which she was dutifully outfitted.

By the time I was a senior in high school, the hierarchy of the who's who (and who's not) had long been established. Much of it had been determined during my sophomore year by Miss Harkness, a tall, round woman with an Irish twinkle in her sea-blue eyes. Miss Harkness wore men's shorts and shirts, had her hair cut in a barber shop and fragranced herself with Old Spice. She headed the Girls' Leaders Club, the most prestigious organization in the school. Once accepted into that group, through tryout and election by Miss Harkness and the existing members, the fortunate newcomer could wear the esteemed green vest over her white gym suit, elevating her status high above that of the other girls. She would assist in gym classes, make the teams for which she tried out and be favored in competitions. Miss Harkness did not like me. The day the tryout results for the Leaders Club were posted was one of the longest and worst I'd ever endured.

The names of the fortunate ones were posted on the gym door. My best friend, Betty Gomez, and I had chatted the entire walk to school about our hopes of making the club. When the school doors opened at 7:30 a.m., we girls all crowded around, holding our breaths, looking for our name on that most important list. Betty, the twins, and all my other friends made it. I did not. Those new members were quickly escorted to the girls' locker room where they were dressed in funny hats, balloons, and silly make-up, their initiation into the club. Amidst the laughter and congratulations filling the hallways that day, I walked from class to class as if in a daze, smiling, trying to act as if it didn't matter to me that I was now on the outside, separated from my friends and sorely rejected. At home the facade continued. I don't think Mom even knew that I had tried out for the club, nor the significance of being denied entry. We never spoke of it.

I did find dignity and status by being accepted into the Advanced Mixed Chorus and by holding office in the Student Council. I had created a place for myself in the society called high school, a place where everyone of teen years must, by law, assemble for the purpose of being educated. But we learned, oh, so much more there.

I had, since entering the public school system in ninth grade, found my way into honors English class. I loved grammar. It was the only thing that made sense to me. I could write fairly well. I could think. My English teachers recognized my aptitude for literature and language and showed their approval. Miss Kennedy, a very thin, straightforward young woman with red-painted lips would give me poems to analyze. I was quite good at that. Mr. McDonough gave me a perfect grade on my presentation of JD Salinger when I performed high points of his works rather than giving the usual oral report about the author. My student nemesis, Tom Lessing, vehemently shouted out, "What was that?" when I finished. Mr. McDonough had to explain to Tom and the class that I had met all the requirements of the assignment, but presented it in an unusual and creative way. Tom did not see the value of my work, but my teacher did, and he praised me for it.

I was mainstreamed into regular classes for all the other subjects until my senior year. My schedule read "Room 101 - Political Theory." With trepidation I entered the room and found a seat. Two teachers entered: Mr. Jack Bilello, a tall dark-haired man with a constant smile, and Mr. Vincent Buscareno, a shorter man with flat-topped hair and black horn-rimmed glasses framing a kind, round face. I looked around the room. Mike Billa, Karen and Catherine Schiebel (the twins), Beatrice Gelato, Tom Lessing—these were all very bright kids! Before class began, I timidly raised my hand. "I think I'm in the wrong class," I said, feeling the discomfort of stares.

"What's your name?" Mr. Bilello asked.

"Grace Papagno," I managed to squeak out. "I'm supposed to be in regular social studies and this is honors."

"Oh, you're right here on the list," Mr. Bilello told me. "Stay a while. I think you'll like it here."

And with that, I became a full-fledged member of the Buscareno/Bilello think- room. It began with Mr. Buscareno's holding up a chair by one leg (a very difficult task) and asking, "What makes this chair to be a chair." Minds spun. Brains awakened. Ideas formed. I loved this! It wasn't long before we were reading Plato's works and comparing them to Aristotle's. Philosophy, anthropology, and social issues were out there for us to discuss and explore.

By the time the first marking period ended, I felt absolutely at home in my new arena of learning. My report card gave credence that I was in the right place - a 95% - excellence! In that first class after the distribution of grades, Karen Schiebel, my former best friend from elementary school and current member of the Girls' Leaders Club, raised her hand. Loudly and unabashed she asked, "I did better on the tests than Grace. Why is it that she has a 95% and I only have a 93%?"

I felt like crawling under the desk and disappearing. My mouth went dry and I couldn't have spoken if I'd been asked to. I felt for certain that I had been discovered! I actually didn't belong in the class, and I would be removed, sent to another, in disgrace.

Mr. Buscareno smiled gently at Karen. "You see, the grade is not only based on test scores, but also on participation. Grace has been thoroughly involved in our debates and discussions. That elevates her grade."

I'd been saved. Mr. Buscareno vouched for me. He was on my side. Karen was not happy at all. I thought of apologizing to her for her lower grade but thought better of it. I let her stew and tried to ignore her. My adventure in political theory continued. We read and discussed and learned.

One day Mr. Buscareno called me to stay after class a moment. "Grace, I have this book I think you'll enjoy. Here, take it. Let me know what you think."

A book! I had enough to do all my homework. I had never been comfortable reading. It seemed each time I sat down to read, Mom would interrupt. "Get up and do something." was her order of the day. Besides, I worked at the bakery after school for three hours each day as well as Saturday and Sunday mornings. "Thanks, Mr. Buscareno." I reluctantly took *Lust for Life* and, at first slowly and then with eagerness, devoured the story and pain of Vincent Van Gogh.

"Oh, Grace," Mr. Buscareno again stopped me. Not another book?

"Here's one I know you'll enjoy." The only part of *The Story of the Trapp Family Singers*, the memoir from which *The Sound of Music* was made, that I didn't like was when Georg died after settling in the United States. I cried so hard, it was difficult to continue reading.

And so as the year went on, Mr. Buscareno filled me with stories of wonder and strength. I now realize that he was teaching me the stuff that parents were supposed to give their children: determination, confidence, and self-worth. His examples were dynamic, and I have used them throughout my life. I also learned during that year that Mr. Buscareno had a wife and two young children, and that he attended Mass each morning before school. I am certain his faith is where he found his calm and strength.

With his fountain pen, he wrote in my yearbook: *Dear Grace, Stay as sweet as you are. Never doubt your ability—you have much to offer. And when you are blue, look for the silver lining and remember the words of your old history teacher. V. Buscareno.*

With the help of a few special teachers, I survived high school: I learned my lessons, got along well with others, found a college. But it was a struggle. Although I lost my best friend to her new popularity, I pretended we were still close. At home, Mom seemed to be constantly sharpening her distain for me. It was the loneliest time of my life.

MODERN BAKERY

SEPTEMBER BROUGHT ME TO MY junior year of high school, my sixteenth birthday and, finally, my working papers. I wanted to find a job to earn more spending money than babysitting afforded me, so I began the long and delicate process of getting Mom to okay the proposition of my working after school.

"Your grades will go down. You'll have no time for homework. No, a job is not a good idea."

"But Mom, I'll get all my work done. It will only be part-time. I need to save money for college."

I really didn't understand why Mom didn't want me to work after school. Perhaps she automatically objected simply because it was something I wanted. She certainly wasn't happy with my company when I was at home. Eventually she relented.

One of the very quiet seniors in my typing class told me that she was thinking of quitting her job at the local bakery because she was preparing to leave for college. I had seen her working there through the window as I passed by sometimes after school. She wore a white cotton uniform and a little white apron. I thought that working at Modern Bakery would be the best, most prestigious job in the world, so I mustered up courage, stopped in, and asked to be hired.

Two sisters ran the place. They were in their mid-forties and very direct. The one I spoke to was Mrs. Ralste, the elder. She questioned me, took my phone number, and told me she'd let me know. When two weeks passed and I hadn't heard, I stopped in again and quietly reminded her about the job. This time the younger, Mrs. Stach, told me that she'd call me. On my third visit, Mrs. Ralste looked me up and down and finally said yes, I could have the job. I was to start on Saturday morning at 11:00 a.m. Filled with joy and trepidation at the prospect of my first real job, I walked the mile home that afternoon, my heart bursting with excitement. I was going to be a bakery girl! Modern Bakery was the wonderful place that had supplied our First Friday breakfasts at OLPH. Once I had been asked to divvy the buns to my classmates. I'd loved it, and now I would get paid for the task!

I arrived promptly at 11:00 a.m. Handing me a white uniform and apron, Mrs. Ralste made it quite clear, in short, curt phrases, that if I were to intended work at 11:00, I should show up about ten minutes ahead of time to prepare. The "early girl" who worked the shift before me would leave exactly at 11:00. Then she led me halfway down the long, dark corridor leading to the back where the delectables were made. The place smelled of sugar and butter, and the floors were dark brown, richly oiled wood. On the right was a very tiny room with a sink and toilet, illuminated by a single bulb on a wire. This is where I was to change into my uniform, which I did quickly, returning to the front to be greeted by Mrs. Stach. She gave me the basic run-down: "These are unmade boxes. When you have time, fold boxes and stack them in the cubbies. You also should brush out the bread racks." She demonstrated sweeping the long-hair brush along the metal holders with her right hand while balancing the elevated rack in her left. She also ran over the prices for me: buns, five cents; coffee rings, sixty-nine cents; cakes, a dollar nineteen.

The bread slicing machines were quite intimidating since, as Mrs. Stach casually told me, "If you let go of the lever and catch your hand, the machine will slice it up. So pay attention."

There was an art to taking hold of the sliced loaf and balancing it vertically in one hand while slipping the waxed bag over it. Tying up cake boxes with string was a talent in itself. I thought I would never master all these tasks and felt quite inept when my first customer arrived. I greeted her with "Hello" and "May I help you?" When she rattled off a litany of products she wanted to buy, I took a swatch of wax paper and carefully pulled apart buns, boxed a coffee cake, and fumbled with the wrapping. Mrs. Stach appeared. "Always keep the flaps outside. No bugs or rain can get in that way. Hold the string in both hands, wrap the string, twist the box, wrap the string again, this time on the other sides, bring up the ends of the string, break it, and tie a double knot." She made it look so easy!

And so I left work at 3:00, tired yet energized, doubtful yet determined. I had made it through my first day, and I *would* learn everything I needed to know.

My work week ran from Wednesday through Friday after school until closing, Saturday from 11:00 a.m. to 3:00 p.m., and Sunday from 6:30 a.m. until 2:00 p.m. Monday and Tuesday the shop was closed. By my calculations, there was enough time on weekday evenings for homework and dating on Friday and Saturday nights. Sunday mornings would be tough but I was tougher, and so my career blossomed.

It was not long before I had the rhythm of the bakery syncopated with my own timing. I could add up product prices in my head, wrap, tie, slice, and bag. Understanding the psyche of my two bosses took some doing. Mrs. Stach, who spent most of her time in the shop, liked to know everything about everyone who came in. She chatted endlessly with customers and frequently tried to wheedle information out of me. I learned how to feign ignorance. Mrs. Ralste, who made and decorated the cakes in the back, was strong, silent, and a little bit frightening. She never smiled, and she barked out orders succinctly. "Get the tray of cakes in from the back!" "Pack a bunch of pound boxes of cookies for Sunday!" Even before her words were acknowledged, she'd turn and disappear into that long corridor to the scorching "back."

When I had been at the bakery for about two months, I found myself trying to keep busy, since only a handful of customers had come into the store. I dusted out the bread and roll bins, removed all items from the bottom cases, and scrubbed dried icing from the glass fronts with ammonia-water. I eliminated crumbs from the two slicing machines. Now I saw my opportunity to have some fun. I quickly cleaned out the front window, carefully dusting the brides and grooms and the shelves on which they waited for weddings. I swept the floors and then made boxes. When I was finished, there was no room for another folded box, nor did a crumb lie anywhere except atop a bun. Now I made my move! I leaned against the bread bin looking bored. When Mrs. Ralste huffed in from the back, she became noticeably irritated by my apparent laziness. "Why are you just standing there?" she growled. "Why don't you do something?"

"There's nothing to do," I replied meekly.

"Dust the bins," she ordered.

"They're dusted," I answered.

"Well then, wash the showcases."

"Washed," I clicked.

"Sweep."

"Done."

"What about boxes?" Mrs. Ralste gazed at the overflowing box cubbies. She stomped to the front looking hard at the shelves and the windows. The entire store was pristine. She looked at me, began to say something and stopped herself, then turned to escape to the back.

That night before I left, Mrs. Ralste emerged from making her last cake and began bagging bread, coffee ring, and buns for me. "Here, these are for you and your family." I do believe she smiled at me, and in my own way I knew I had broken into the hard shell she wore over her delicate heart. I felt pride in having won Mrs. Ralste's respect. Though we never spoke of it, we were friends after that day.

I worked for two years at the very old fashioned Modern Bakery. On graduation day, I was up at 5:00 and at the shop before 6:00 in the morning. I had explained to Mrs. Ralste and Mrs. Stach that I'd have to leave by noon to attend my graduation ceremony at 1:30. As I called down the corridor that I was leaving, Mrs. Ralste hollered, "Just wait a minute!"

I panicked. *What does she want? I explained why I had to leave early. I can't be late for graduation.*

Mrs. Ralste appeared from the back with a giant ten-inch strawberry shortcake—the fresh whipped cream at least an inch thick, the entire cake covered in halved, magnificently luscious strawberries. "Here. Happy Graduation," she said, smiling at me.

"Oh Mrs. Ralste, it's beautiful! My favorite! You made it special for me?"

"Aw, go on. Don't be late." She drew the attention away from herself, as was her way. It was the best graduation present I could think of. Shortly after that, on the night of my senior prom, I made it a point to stop to see Mrs. Ralste before my date picked me up. She said I looked pretty.

After I'd left Modern Bakery for college, I continued to stop in to say hello to the sisters. When some years had passed, I learned that Mrs. Ralste was sick with cancer, and for the first time, I was invited to her home upstairs from the shop. There, without words, I said goodbye to my boss, my friend, my role model. She died not long after that.

I continue to visit Mrs. Stach at the bakery. She's in her mid-eighties and still wants to know everything about everyone. The place still smells like sugar and butter. I still go into the small kitchen behind the shop and have coffee and a buttered roll with her. We laugh and reminisce about a sweet time in a wonderful old place where I will always belong—Modern Bakery.

COLLEGE DAYS

MY COLLEGE EXPERIENCE ENCOMPASSED far more than what I learned from new-found friendships and in classes. I acquired tenacity and the kind of determination I'd only witnessed in my favorite characters of movies and books. I learned to stand undauntedly on my own and to move forward confidently toward my goals.

Mom informed me that I would be going to Oneonta State College; that's where Carole was at the time, so it was good enough for me. Carole, in her typically insensitive fashion, told me that if I persisted in my "casual" high school study habits, I would never make the grade in college. I'd never had to pore over books the way that Carole did in order to earn the same high grades. Her words stuck with me, filling me with even more self-doubt than I'd had before, and I wondered if I would even be able to manage college.

Since Mom was busy with work and looking after the house, I had to somehow make my way up to the college during July before school began in order to set up my freshman schedule. I learned that Sue Trayes, a friendly girl in my senior English class, would be traveling there with her mom, so I asked if I could go along with them. It was a long drive, but Mrs. Trayes was quite capable of making the trip up and back. We stayed overnight in a small motel, and I paid my way with money I'd earned at the bakery. My resulting schedule began each day with 8:00 a.m. classes, the only ones remaining after the upper classmen had grabbed the more popular ones. I was not looking forward to early rising.

One September afternoon, Mom and Dad dropped Carole and me at the Oneonta campus, she at the old Morris Hall where she'd elected to live and I at Ford Hall, a new building on top of the hill on which the campus lay. I'd never been away from home before and felt quite insignificant when Mom announced, "Okay, now you're on your own. We're leaving. Goodbye." She left a bit of cake she'd baked and which we'd snacked on at lunch time during the five-hour ride upstate. I met my roommate who, I learned, had a boyfriend with whom she spent most of her free time and ate all her meals. She had a whiney voice which made her absence easier to take. Our room was one of three small bedrooms which opened onto a large "living room" housing six desks, one for each of us in the suite. Adjoining this room was a bathroom that we shared. I soon discovered that two of my suitemates were from my high school, girls with whom I had nothing in common and rarely, if ever, spoke with at home. The other two were also from Long Island.

When Mom and Dad arrived home many hours later, Mom called me, blithely announcing, "Oh, I forgot it was your birthday. How silly. Happy Birthday. That cake was your birthday cake," and with a chuckle, she hung up the phone. Choking back tears, I was busying myself with unpacking when Kathy, an upper classman who roomed next door, came in to greet us. She heard that it was my eighteenth birthday, and I suspect she sensed my loneliness. With a huge grin of delight, Kathy insisted that I join her on a short trip downtown for my first legal beer. I thought she was wonderful. I settled in and college life began. I found people here and there to chat with, to eat with, but no deep friendships developed.

I purchased all the books my professors required, but when classes began, I found that I could not figure out what to read and when to read it, which chapters had to do with which lecture. No one provided me with an outline or explained what was expected. I took notes, attended classes, and learned halfway through the semester that I had fallen fearfully behind in my reading.

I had no idea then how to budget my time. My friends who lived across the hall rushed a sorority, but I remained an "independent," as we were called. I had no time for sorority life, and I knew that I would never fit into a giggly girls' group that seemed silly to me. What was meaningful and probably kept me going throughout my college years was the Women's Glee Club.

My sister Carole had failed to make the Glee Club until her sophomore year. She sang in a group for which there was no audition her freshman year, and she assumed I would follow the same path. Shortly after classes had begun, when I signed up to try out for the Glee Club, I was terrified. I had never auditioned for anything before nor had I ever sung alone. When I awoke that morning, my situation became desperate. I realized that I'd caught a cold. I was congested, and my voice was noticeably strained and distorted. I couldn't hear very well. I remember going into my audition with wobbly knees and dashed hopes of doing well. Mr. B, as Charles Burnsworth, the director, was known, invited me into a large choral room. He was a handsome man in his mid-thirties with sandy brown hair and a very pleasant disposition. A senior girl named Reggie sat at the piano. Mr. B asked me to sing a bit of a well-known song while Reggie accompanied me. Then he tested my range, which was diminished considerably by my cold. He played various intervals of three to five notes and asked me to sing them, measuring my listening ear. By the time I left the audition, I was certain that I'd failed and had nowhere to go with my disappointment but to my sister, who was casual if not callous. "Well, you'll have to sing with the Choraleers for a year like I did, and then try again," she said and humpfed.

A few days later I received a phone call from Mr. B telling me that I had indeed, made the Glee Club! I was in, and the thought of singing in this group made me deliriously happy. When I told Carole, she didn't seem particularly pleased and humpfed again. I could only imagine what she was thinking.

Glee Club rehearsals kept me going. We practiced two hours each Monday evening and one hour at lunchtime on Tuesdays and Thursdays for which we were awarded a class credit each semester. My experiences singing classical and secular pieces with orchestras and men's choruses throughout New York State and traveling on tour were in themselves an education. I felt elevated to the height of the masters. I learned to read music and to follow a conductor. I loved singing. At the beginning of my second semester, Mr. B called me into his office. I had no idea what he wanted to say to me, and my expectations were low. I was astounded when he asked me to become a member of The Jongleurs, a women's octet which sang madrigals and jazz pieces. I was delighted; Carole was demoralized. I sang on.

Throughout my freshman year, I seemed to flourish in my humanities, English, and literature classes but did not do well in the sciences. I'd enrolled in an education class, thinking that I would be an elementary school teacher when I graduated. During my first semester as an education major, I was expected to teach a class at the Bugbee Elementary School, located at the foot of the hill on which the college stood. After spending hours preparing a trial lesson for a first grade class, I found the little buggers had an attention span of about a minute, and I'd lost them long before I could capture their attention. When their regular teacher addressed us college students, she warned, "If you didn't love doing this today, you'd better change your major." With that sage advice, I walked up the hill directly to the Dean of Students' office in the Administration Building to change my major to English with a minor in education. With this degree I could teach at the secondary level for which I'd be more suited. Happily, the bulk of my future courses would be in literature; unhappily, I still needed to pass chemistry, Spanish I and II, microbiology, and political science. Although I worked hard at these courses, even pulling all-nighters to study for tests, I found myself failing. I sought help from my college counselor whose solution was to hand me a book entitled *The SQ3R Method of Learning*. I never became comfortable with the "survey, question, read, recite, and review" method. What I really needed, and lacked, was someone to believe in me. My college experience, a journey of bends and brakes, twists and turns, had just begun, and I was about to learn exactly who and what I was and what I was capable of accomplishing.

WHEN I BECAME QUEEN

IT WAS EARLY SEPTEMBER. The morning mountain air was clear and cool, and I breathed it deeply as I strutted across the Oneonta State campus toward Morris Hall. Though I had just turned eighteen years old, I knew I was "grown-up." Here I was a college freshman, a coed, away from home and on my own, about to get my first work-study job that would afford me a little spending money and a lot of independence.

Up the broad steps and into the oldest residence on campus I walked assuredly. The information attendant directed me to follow the long hall to the stairway leading down to the dining hall. My steps echoed off the heavy cream-colored walls.

I found a grand room lined with folded tables and molded plastic chairs in various garish colors. The back wall, composed entirely of windows, revealed rolling lawns, pine trees, and a distant mountain. We freshmen had arrived early for orientation, so the upperclassmen who would soon dine in this hall were not yet on campus. There was a ghostly air about the place.

Slowly I made my way past a vacant serving line and into the kitchen. Mammoth stoves, a wall-sized oven, and an electric mixer that stood my height confronted me as I entered this epicurean cavern. In the far corner a light shown out of a tiny office. "Hello!" I gently called, walking toward the light.

"Yeah?" A ruddy-faced, slightly balding red head poked out the doorway.

"Are you Charlie?" I wondered if this was the head of the dining hall, the man whom I had been told to ask for a job.

"Yeah, what can I do for you?" He was in his mid-thirties, carrying a few extra pounds that were the result, no doubt, of his constant interaction with food.

"Hi, Charlie, my name is Grace. I was told that you had work-study jobs.

"Oh, yeah. Sorry, I gave out the last one yesterday.

The idea of not getting a job hadn't crossed my mind. "You mean there are absolutely no positions left? Nothing?" My heart began to thud, and I could feel my lower lip quiver. *Don't you dare cry*, I scolded myself.

"The only place I have left is for a dishwasher."

"I'll take it," I said quickly without giving it a thought.

"You can't. It's for a dishwasher." Charlie looked at me strangely.

"I don't understand. Why can't I have the job?"

"Well, 'cause you're a girl." He looked at me as if I must have been witless not to have understood that fact before asking.

"Wait a minute." I could feel my back straighten and my voice strengthen. "You mean to tell me that because I'm a girl, the reason that I've *had* to wash dishes my entire life, is now the reason that I can't wash dishes?" I simply couldn't understand the logic here.

"Well, yeah. It's dirty and hot in the dishroom. The racks of glasses are heavy. You have to lift them into and take them out of the dishwashers. A girl can't do that."

"I'll take the job, Charlie. I can handle it. You'll see. I need this job, and I'm taking it. There's no way I'm going to be forced out of having spending money because I'm a girl!"

There was a moment between us. Then Charlie made his decision. "Okay, then. I hope you can handle it."

"I can. You'll see." I stood still for a moment. I'd won my battle but still had to face the war.

"You start Monday morning. Breakfast. Be here at 6:30. See you then." Charlie returned to his office work, and I left to meet up with my new friends.

Charlie never doubted me after that day. I made sure of it. The following Monday morning I arrived, in the dark, to work. I donned the long, white apron and withstood the stares of all the guys I would be working with. But I soon learned how to run the dishroom.

When they'd finished their breakfast, students would place their trays, filled with half-eaten oatmeal and toast, eggs and ham, hash and fritters, through an arch onto a stainless steel counter. My job was to pull in the tray, pick up the plate, clear all the food debris into a garbage disposal, place the plate and tray onto the slowly marching conveyer belt of the dishwasher, upend glasses and cups into their proper racks above the counter, and place silverware in cylindrical bins on the right. When the cup and glass racks were full, I'd lift the racks down and place them onto the belt. I did the same with the silverware bins.

When I saw the upperclassmen giving each other looks and shaking their heads, I became even more determined not to be too weak for the job. Although the racks were exceedingly heavy, my high school work at the bakery had prepared me. Carrying eight layer cakes on a tray above my shoulder and putting them into the baker's cabinet was similar to swinging a rack of glasses over and placing it onto the conveyer belt. I never once allowed any of the guys to help me; I had to carry my own weight.

For a few weeks, I could see student diners' heads lowering to peer through the arch when they delivered their used trays filled with the aftermath of meals. They may have wondered whose little hands these were, so efficiently cleaning and dividing the dishes.

I knew I had won my case with Charlie and the guys when, one day, Christian called through the arch at a curious student, "You wanna know who that is? Why it's Gracie, Queen of the Dishroom!" All my dishwashing gang cheered! I felt my face flush, and I smiled at them. I had been accepted! It was one of my finest moments. After that we were a team. We all helped each other out, and no one was better or worse than another. My new nickname stuck; in Morris Hall I was called Queenie.

At a recent college reunion, I stepped back into the room where I once worked. There, young women clanged dishes and cups side by side with young men. There was no gender division; they all worked casually together. I smiled to myself, thinking that way back in 1966, one young woman had fought for the right to be equal to the men and won—and was thereby elevated to royalty.

NIGHT AT THE COFFEE HOUSE

DURING MY FIRST YEAR at the State University College at Oneonta I befriended Bob, an easy-going, preppy-styled freshman who had the sweet job of working the events at Morris Hall, the campus social center. This included being in charge of the new Coffee House set up in the basement of Old Main, the original Normal School at Oneonta situated at the foot of the hill.

Each Saturday night entertainment was presented there. I remember seeing a bright young country singer who did a great job accompanying himself on the guitar. His name was John Denver, and none of us had heard of him yet.

Bob and I were not dating, but we did hang out together frequently. Most of the time I accompanied him to the Coffee House on Saturday nights. Early one of those evenings, Bob seemed to be in a state of panic when I arrived at Morris Hall, intending to have dinner and then go to Old Main for the show. "My singer has cancelled at the last minute," Bob blurted at me. "I have no one to go on."

We considered the situation, and in a way typical to us, we began canvassing the crowd entering the Morris Hall cafeteria for dinner. "Do you sing? Play an instrument? Have any kind of an act?" We asked the same questions of total strangers as well as students we knew. One eager, good-looking young man, I think he was a junior, answered, "Yeah, I play the harmonica."

"Really? Could you perform at the Coffee House tonight at seven?"

"Sure. I'll eat and then get my stuff. I'll meet you there a little before seven to set up."

We were saved! Reveling in our good fortune at finding a replacement so fast, Bob and I took a leisurely dinner at Morris Hall and moseyed over to the Coffee House. As we descended the shadowed stairway into the low, beamed-ceiling room, our eyes took a moment to acclimatize to the dimness. Large, heavy wooden tables with benches filled the area, and a makeshift stage stood at the front of the space. There Brian, our savior, met us and set up the stool, mike, and music stand. The audience began arriving, ordered beverages and we were on. Bob introduced Brian and settled close to me, our shoulders touching, to enjoy the show.

At first, we thought there was a problem with the mike. Our bodies tensed. The sound of a deep inhale was followed by an ungodly dissonance. Notes smashed into each other between breaths that were as loud as the notes. Could this be the "act" Brian had promised? After a paralyzed moment, I whispered to Bob, "It sounds like open-heart surgery gone wrong," and our shoulders began to shake helplessly as we tried to stifle our laughter. We were simultaneously panic-stricken and laughing hysterically. Heat steamed off the back of my neck. We had to think fast, but first we had to compose ourselves enough to speak coherently.

"Do you know anyone?" Bob whispered to me.

My mind raced through my acquaintances and friends. "Yeah, I think Maryellen Shaw is on campus with her boyfriend visiting this weekend. She's in the Glee Club with me, and she's really good on guitar."

Bob and I snuck out to find the phone in the hallway, and I hastily made the call. "Hi Maryellen, so glad you're in. We have a situation here at the Coffee House and could really use some music. Can you come? Sure, he can do it with you. Great! As soon as you can!"

"She's on her way with John. They'll do a show together," I assured Bob, and we tiptoed back into the room.

Bob and I sat together in horror as the painful noises continued:

magnified breath followed by cacophonous harmonica. Tears flowed from our eyes as we stifled laughter, invisible, we hoped, in the darkness.

When Maryellen finally arrived, I had never been happier to see anyone. Bob thanked Brian for his "music" and wrapped up the "act" while Maryellen and John set up. Within minutes, skillful guitar music and soaring harmonies filled the Coffee House. Bob and I were saved, and the crowd gratefully tapped, nodded and hummed along with the music.

In retrospect, it seems to me that the entire night was exceptionally entertaining. It was one that I remember still, always laughing aloud at the thought of those days of youth and friendship, rough spots and skin-of-our-teeth successes.

THAT RIDE WITH DAD

SHORTLY AFTER ARRIVING HOME after my freshman year, I received the letter I'd expected. I was asked not to return to Oneonta State since my grades were not in keeping with their standards. It was over. A hollow feeling rushed through me as I handed the letter to Mom and left the kitchen. I think my family passed the letter around among themselves, but no one spoke of it or of my disgrace.

I continued working at the little town bay beach where I was expected to mind the nurse's station. My job was chiefly to remove splinters from little fingers and give out Band-aids. It was still early in June when Daddy announced that we were going to Uncle Dom's restaurant for dinner. I was a little surprised when Daddy asked me to ride with him in his car and meet the rest of the family there. I knew that the ride would take about forty-five minutes, and I was pleased to have some rare alone time with Dad. I didn't know what he had planned, but this ride gave Daddy the chance he wanted. "Grace, why don't you go to Nassau Community College for a while?" he said casually as he merged onto Southern State Parkway.

"No, Daddy. I tried and I really worked hard. I'm just not made to go to college."

"But Grace," he spoke softly in the voice I could always trust, "you're the smart one. Just go at night. Find a job to work at during the day. You can take any classes you like and see if it makes a difference. Do it for me." Ah, those were the clinching words. What wouldn't I do for my father?

"Okay, I really don't want to, but I'll try it, Daddy. For you. But if I don't like it, I'm not going to finish."

And with that, I enrolled at Nassau Community College night courses for the fall semester. I took American Literature I, English Literature I, and music appreciation, courses I hoped I would enjoy and which would be accepted for credit when and if I returned to Oneonta, as I was covertly advised by Mr. B., who never lost faith in me.

Mom found me a job through someone with whom she worked. I was to be a secretary to an architect in Amityville, Robert D. Donohue. There I learned that typing letters was not my forte. I was using a typewriter which meant every blunder was a do-over. I loved organizing the office and working with the classical British type, Robert Donohue, and his sidekick, the sweet and loveable Carl Hagen, but a career as a secretary was clearly not for me. On Mondays, Wednesdays, and Fridays when I was scheduled for evening classes, I would wake up early, walk from home up to Montauk Highway, take the long ride to Amityville on the public bus, walk past large, old houses the mile from Montauk Highway where the bus had let me off, north to the village of Amityville and into the ancient Triangle Building's second floor to the office of Robert Donohue, Architect. The old steps loudly creaked my arrival each day, so being on time was important. Daddy left his car parked on the adjacent street after his early morning golf game and rode with a friend to work and then home again. He never once complained about this inconvenience. After work at 5:00, I drove Daddy's blue Cutlass the fifteen miles to Nassau Community College.

The college, located on what had been Mitchel Field, an American Air Force Base renowned as the place where Charles Lindberg began his transatlantic flight, had all the charm I'd expected of a place noted in American history. Nervously, I parked Dad's car and made my way toward the cluster of buildings that were now the college. This was my make-or-break chance.

I found the cafeteria where I'd planned to have a cup of coffee, but after noticing the wide selection of roasts, potatoes, vegetables, and salads offered, I decided to have my dinner there each week. It wasn't long before I'd made some friends with whom I ate. My three classes ran from 7:00 p.m. through 9:45 p.m., and then I would trek back to the car and drive home, arriving there by 10:30 p.m. Because two of my three classes concerned literature, I found myself reading every possible minute. I ate corn flakes over George Gordon, Lord Byron and a sandwich with James Fennimore Cooper; I read each evening in bed; I read during the weekends. I found the professors at Nassau utterly inspiring and was fascinated by their every word. Mr. Jenkins was bright with a dry sense of humor that I grew to appreciate along with the early American novelists. Dr. George A. Brenner wore a tie clasp with his initials that did not go unnoticed as he spoke on and on about the magnificence of the English poets. Sweet, wonderful Dr. Glickman was so clear about the elements of music that I learned to recognize many aspects of a musical piece. Even as the winter wind outside rattled the old barracks in which our class was held, I could distinguish the tempo, instruments, and harmonies emanating from the record as Dr. Glickman dropped the needle onto the vinyl at random. Each of my teachers gave his students a list of authors and works to have read by class time, which was an enormous help to me and something lacking at Oneonta. Many evenings the discussion from class would continue as a group of us strolled to our cars debating one point or another, tired yet energized by our ideas. I was motivated, delighted, and actually excited about learning!

It came to me one evening in the cafeteria, while considering the many types of people eating there, that night school was the place where people on their way up and those on their way down, academically, met. I was determined to be one who moved up.

My first test, one in English Literature, required me to answer three of five essays. I thought I'd done well but was flabbergasted when I saw the D at the top of the page. "*No one flunks out of night school,*" I muttered to myself on the ride home that night. This would not happen to me again. I had to change my tactics, and so besides taking notes and listening attentively, I reread my notes each evening before sleep. It was as if I'd memorized my notebook without trying. The evening before Dr. Brenner's next test, I did not study. I did not open a book. I went to the movies with my sister, Margie. Amazingly, I scored an A+ and after that night, I never attained anything less than an A in any course during both fall and spring semesters. I even aced modern math, a course that I took the following summer along with three other courses. I had actually completed a full year's worth of credits, 30 in all, at night school! By working during the days, I was able to repay my student loan from my freshman year and also pay Nassau Community College as I went.

My perfect 4.0 cumulative average at Nassau paved an easy access for me to return to Oneonta. I suppose that I could have entered any state school without question, but I felt the need to prove, both to myself and to those who'd seen me fail, that I could succeed there. Although the dean wouldn't apply my perfect grades toward my average at Oneonta, I didn't lose any credits from the full year earned at Nassau, and so I reentered as a junior. Once again I sang in the Women's Glee Club. I enrolled primarily in literature classes and in the spring headed up the grand stairway to the new Administration Building into the Dean of Students' office to set up my plan to student teach the following spring. "My dear," the older and dignified Kate Hobbie offered apathetically, "we do not offer secondary student teaching in the spring. You'll have to add an extra semester to complete your degree."

An extra semester was, for me, out of the question. I was paying my own way, and another five months of room and board plus courses was not in my plan. I phoned home, told them that I would be spending the summer at Oneonta, found an apartment and took the necessary courses that preceded student teaching. In September I was assigned to a small rural school district where I became *the* high school English teacher, taking on the 9th through 12th grade classes. I learned from an expert teacher, the helpful Jim Cowden, and was amused that some of my students were my own age. It required countless hours of work, but my student teaching experience was amazing, and I knew that I was destined to be a teacher. I returned to classes in November for quarter courses, the follow-up to student teaching, and by Christmas break I had earned my degree graduating with honors.

I'd learned that with determination, an unfailing look to the future, and concentration on my goals, I could do anything. I was hired by a local school district the week I arrived home. I had a job. Strangely enough, my friends who had not flunked out, graduated six months after me, and by that time the teaching market had dried up. They could not find jobs. I had been led on a journey of disappointment, disgrace, hard work, and finally good fortune. I realized that even when a situation seemed hopeless, it might offer benefits that I could not see at the moment, a lesson I've never forgotten and continue to live by.

Almost forty years later, after completing a wonderful thirty-four-year career teaching English, I received a phone call from Stephanie who was then in her junior year at university. "Hi, Mom, you have to come here to give a one hour lecture on time management to my business fraternity. Well, it's called a fraternity but it's open to guys and girls. You're an expert, Mom, and the kids will love you. It's my job to find a presentation for the group, and I know that you're the best. You can come on either Wednesday or Friday of next week, so which will it be?"

Imagine that!

TEACHING
MICHAEL B.

I HAD BEEN TEACHING FOR A few years —*an old-timer*, I thought. The rhythm of junior high school set a comfortable tempo for me, and I usually had fun both teaching my lessons and with the students individually. Although I insisted that the job be done well and completely, my antics—singing, dancing, acting out characters—made the learning fun for all, and so the kids didn't complain, mostly, except for Patricia, in that terrible eighth period class. She complained about everything and everybody. I took her behavior with a grain of salt. I had met her mother at open school night and, in her case, it was a dark, cranky, unmannerly oak tree giving example to this surly thirteen-year-old acorn.

Although Patricia was neither a particularly pretty nor personable girl, she had attracted the attention of Michael B., who sat near her. They shared confidences and conversations while the rest of us carried on with the lesson of the day. My tactic with such alliances was to divide and conquer. Usually by taking one of the miscreants aside and speaking sweetly, I would win the culprit over to my side, and shortly thereafter, the other would follow. But that wasn't the case this time.

One Friday afternoon in early spring, Patricia and Michael were feeling the spirit of the season especially strongly. No amount of coaxing quieted them. Finally, I invited Michael into my "office," which was outside the classroom in the hallway. There I quietly asked, "Michael, is anything wrong?"

"No," he said with a shrug.

"Well then, what's all the ruckus about?"

"Nothin'," was all he uttered.

I reached out to fold Michael's hands gently into mine and held them as I spoke. "Michael, it's really difficult to go on with the class when ...."

With that, and I never saw it coming, Michael hauled off and punched me in the face. I was stunned. The hall monitor, another teacher, jumped out of his seat and pulled Michael away from me. He called the office for coverage and suggested I go to the faculty room.

My mind raced with what had just happened. I had never experienced this kind of behavior by a student. I was rather popular with the kids. What had gone wrong?

The principal was quick to ask, "Do you want to press charges?"

"Charges? What kind of charges? What are you talking about?"

"This was an assault. You can press charges if you want to."

"No. No charges."

"Michael's parents are coming up. I called them. They're stopping at church first to pray. Why don't you go home?"

Still in a fog and somewhat in pain, I drove home, my mind reeling. *I don't think I should teach any more. I don't think I can. It's obvious I've lost some sensitivity to my students.* The doubts came fast and hard.

That night my friend and coworker, Eddie Ryan, came to my house to take me out for a beer. He'd never done that before or after. We talked about the incident, and Eddie explained that Michael was a strange-thinking punk-type kid who was on Eddie's football team. Over and over, Eddie told me not to consider quitting. I was a great teacher and shouldn't be set off-track by one nasty kid.

I did return to school that Monday morning and found Michael had been moved to another class. Patricia went on and on about the incident, but I ignored her, and after some time, life returned to normal.

Five years later, after my daughter Stephanie was born, I was transferred to the high school. Learning the preps for three new classes was challenging, but after the first year I found great joy in teaching juniors and seniors and worked happily at that level for many years. I had been given a desk and a file cabinet in the little English office which also served as a book storage room. There Irene Miller, the department chairperson, and I worked quietly and peacefully each third period.

One day a strikingly handsome young man entered the room. He held a bouquet of flowers. "I'm here to see Ms. Papagno."

I stood and looked squarely at him. As if by magic, I recognized him. "Yes, Michael?"

"I've come to apologize."

"I'm listening." I was not going to give into him so easily.

"You see, a year ago I was in a near-fatal car accident. I went through the windshield and should have died. I spent six months in the hospital. It was there that I thought of all the things I should do in my life to make things right. I thought of you, and I knew that I had to apologize to you—and to thank you."

"Thank me? What do you have to thank me for?" I asked finally, softening toward him.

"You never pressed charges. If you had, I would have had a record. You see, I work for the FBI, and I would never have been accepted there with a record. Actually, you taught me a lot."

Irene sat incredulous witnessing Michael's confession.

"Well then, Michael, I accept your apology, and you are welcome." He walked toward me, handed me the bouquet and gave me a hug.

Sometimes it takes a while for a situation to resolve itself. Teaching Michael B. took over fifteen years. The reward and satisfaction that I'd done my job and was truly a good teacher was well worth the wait.

NORTHVILLE

MOST PEOPLE DRIVE RIGHT BY the tiny town of Northville, which lies hidden within the Adirondack Mountains. Travelers find their way to the famous Lake George, but few realize they've come so close to my family's retreat from the modern world. My dad discovered Northville when his work for the NY Racing Association brought him to Saratoga, NY. During his first year working there, Dad commuted home to Long Island each weekend. He and Mom missed each other very much, since it was the first time they'd been separated in their twenty-five-year marriage. When Dad learned from his colleagues that they and their families rented little lakeside cabins, he told Mom about the "campsites," as they were called, and for the next six years, they spent the month of August "vacationing" in the mountains. Mom took a leave from her job, packed home-making items, and trekked with Dad to Lakewood Cottages. Mom found immense pleasure in the relaxed, countrified life she encountered in her little cabin on Northville Lake. She loved to go exploring antique shops in the mornings while the mountain air was still chilled from the previous night. By noon she was back at the cottage in her bathing suit, which she wore preparing and serving lunch. Mom sat with her new lady friends whose husbands all worked with Dad. They'd knit, read, and swim in the pristine lake, always chatting. When the men arrived back at the camp, the families would eat their dinners and then all meet on the beach for a campfire, beach volleyball and laughter.

By the time our parents had discovered Northville, my sisters and I were almost adults. We loved going to the cabin, and each of us joined Mom and Dad there for a week or more. Walking up the long drive to the street, following the edge of the lake, and crossing the little bridge, I would make my way to the village.

There really wasn't much there: the old hardware store that carried just about everything, an abandoned movie theater, a laundromat, a Chinese takeout, a pizza parlor, a barber shop, the Grand Union grocery, and a McCrory's Five and Ten Cent Store. I'd walk to McCrory's and comb the place for great finds, always winding up at Stewart's Ice Cream store afterward for a cone. I brought my bicycle to our little town so I could explore each street, both in the morning and after dinner, when the folks sitting on the front porches of their old houses waved as I rode by.

Mom, my sisters, and I usually made a special trip to the Old Barn two towns down, over the Bachelorville Bridge, toward Broadalbin. It was owned by two middle-aged women who would open the doors and allow us to sift through the junk, unearthing magnificent treasures all morning long.

There were rowboats at Lakewood Cottages, and I usually found someone who wanted to go for a row. At the far end of the lake we'd pass schoolboys diving off the small bridge into the deep, clear water. I kept my swimming to the area in front of our cabin where there was activity. I'd heard of a very, very large turtle living in the lake and I wanted no part of meeting with him.

I even enjoyed a quiet walk with Mom one evening there in Northville, just the two of us, on lonely meandering roads. These were peaceful times filled with joy, but they ended abruptly the awful summer when Dad died.

THE STORM

"OF COURSE I WANT A PIECE OF CAKE!" Why was Mom bothering to ask? She had baked German coffee cake at Bridget's request, for her twenty-third birthday. It was the family custom to request the dinner and cake of your choice on your birthday, and even though we kids had all moved out on our own, our family still gathered for these celebrations.

We made cute remarks to Bridget about her April Fool's birthday. She had grown immune to the jokes and by now just smiled along with the rest of us.

"Daddy, you know, you look a little yellow," Bridget noticed while pouring coffee into his cup.

"Yeah. I have an appointment with Dr. Samak next week to see what's going on. I'll have a little ice cream with my cake." And with that, the conversation diverted to dessert and gifts and the warming trend of the weather that we'd all longed for.

By the time my birthday arrived in September, my seventh year as an English teacher had begun smoothly, and the fear of lesson plans and the newness of the profession had worn off. "The roast beef was perfect, Mom. How do you get the potatoes crunchy on the outside and soft on the inside?" Even when Mom told me exactly how she prepared my favorite meal, the prospect of replicating it seemed impossible to me.

"So what's going on with the doctor?" I asked Daddy over cake and coffee. Your color looks better."

"Oh, Dr. Samak is sending me to an expert on exotic diseases. Seems this peach fuzz that's developed on my face and the yellowness might have been caused by something I picked up when your mother and I vacationed in Colombia last January." Daddy gave no visible sign of how he felt about the new theory. "We'll just have to see what's what. Now pass me one of those brownies. Who the heck ever heard of brownies as birthday cake?"

"Mom's are the best in the world! They're my favorite, and it's my birthday." I smiled at my family as we celebrated my twenty-seventh year.

It was around Christmastime when I followed Dad back into the kitchen after dinner. He removed a large, plastic beverage container from the refrigerator and poured some of the milky contents into a glass. Sourly he drank it.

"What's this?" I asked.

"I have to go for some tests. This is dye. They're going to track my system to see what they can find." He said nothing more. His complexion and the light, barely noticeable fuzzy hair that covered his face had not changed since the summer.

"Daddy, I'm scared. What if something happens to you?" I whispered the unthinkable words aloud for the first time. The dimmed antique lamp cast a warm glow over both of us.

"Nothing's going to happen to me," he said firmly, and our conversation was ended. Daddy never spoke of unpleasant things and rarely about himself.

I learned later that Daddy was an outpatient at Memorial Sloan Kettering Hospital. *Cancer. Sloan Kettering meant cancer. Do they think my dad—my strong, handsome, charming, invincible dad—has cancer? Daddy has only been sick once. Once! And he got over that in two days!* It seemed that we were on some surreal roller-coaster ride, and we waited in hushed silence for the ride to end. But it didn't end. The downward spiral of my dad's health gained momentum as my family pretended that nothing was happening; the deadly silence pounded in my ears.

The February 25th celebration of Daddy's birthday was lighthearted. The camera that had been inserted into his pancreas during the latest test revealed no tumor, nothing abnormal. No cancer! Surely Daddy would recover from this mysterious ailment.

But Mom's treatment of Daddy subtly changed. She no longer made demands of him. She found nothing in the house that needed his attention—no rooms to be painted, no moldings to be replaced, no drains to be cleaned. She spent all her free time with him, in his immediate company. There was an ominous air to it, and I went through the motions of normalcy while watching all the hints of change.

Pretending that no storm existed in their lives, Mom and Dad caravanned their two cars toward their annual August respite in our camp in Northville near Saratoga. At the same time, somewhere off the coast of Africa, another storm began brewing. A tropical depression had been spotted. It moved quickly across the Atlantic Ocean and positioned itself near the Bahamas. Bridget, Margie and I would keep an eye on the house; we all lived nearby Mom and Dad's.

On August 7th, when that storm attained hurricane status, our family home was smashed by its own natural disaster. Mom and Dad returned after only a week in Northville. With few words and cautious movement, our world changed forever. I received a phone call. Daddy was in the hospital. He'd said to Mom, "I can't do it anymore. Let's go home."

When I arrived at the house, the rains and winds had begun. Bridget and Margie met me there, and together we tried to determine what was going on. Mom was casually dusting the dining room. "The hospital will find out what exactly is wrong with your father. I'm going back upstate. He can join me there as soon as he's released."

Bridget looked to Margie and then to me.

"But Mom, there's a hurricane coming. Maybe you should wait awhile," Margie tried to reason with her.

"No, it's fine. I'm going back. He'll meet me as soon as he's well." Mom continued her usual routine while everything around her was in danger. She was determined to return to her vacation spot as if being there would ensure safety.

Margie, Bridget and I felt helpless. There was no one to lead us out of this dilemma. I turned to Mom. "Okay." I had decided. "I'll go with you. But can't we wait until tomorrow when we've both had a night's sleep, and I've had time to get a few things from my apartment?"

This idea appealed to Mom, and the following morning through wind-swept rain, we drove together north the five hours to our upstate retreat while the hurricane named Belle, now classified as a major hurricane, headed up the Atlantic coast toward home.

It was about two o'clock on Sunday the 8th of August when Mom and I stepped onto the soft pine-needle blanket that covered the grounds around our cabin. I had only a small travel bag. Mom's things remained in the cabin from the previous morning. There was only small talk between us during the ride. Mostly we played the radio. There was soothing music mixed with anxious weather updates. Cautiously neutral, I was hoping Mom would rethink the situation.

We decided to walk to town for some milk; although the sky was dark with clouds, there was no rain. We took the long road—up the back hill and down through the village. It seems Mom had ordered a ceramic frog for me from a local woman who made such things. We picked it up and continued to the Grand Union. The walk back was short and quiet. *What must she be thinking?* I wondered.

Mom made us chicken for dinner, and she and I listened to her black portable radio with its wobbly antenna. Belle was strengthening. We tried to play Scrabble and turned in early.

Monday morning brought dark clouds and wind, a summer camper's ingredients for boredom. We decided to drive to the laundromat to take care of last week's clothes and bed linens. We called home from the public telephone in town. Margie answered and reported that Dad had stabilized. The hurricane was due that evening, headed straight for the center of Long Island's south shore. Mom looked at me. "What am I doing here?" Reality had caught up with her.

"Mom, do you want to go home?" I was gentle with her.

She nodded.

"Okay. We can't go today; we'd be driving directly into the storm. We'll pack up everything into the two cars and head home tomorrow morning."

She agreed, and in a requiem for our summer place where we had laughed and swum and played volleyball for so many years, we silently and ceremonially cleared all traces of our family from the little red cabin in the woods.

The rain didn't begin until after dinner. Luckily, we'd packed all the boxes of bed linens and towels, food and clothing, Daddy's golf clubs and board games into the cars before the deluge. That night, shortly after midnight, Belle hit Babylon, our neighboring town. Water covered the streets, and power was out all along the southern coast of the Long Island. I had to get Mom home safely, and she had to drive one of the cars.

"Mom, are you okay to drive?" I was quiet and caring.

"Yes, I'm okay."

"Alright. You'll just have to follow me. I'll lead. We'll go slowly. If the water gets too high, we'll pull over at some motel and stay until we can get through. Let's play it by ear."

She agreed quietly.

Early Tuesday morning, we ate our breakfast cereal. I waited in the screened porch while Mom gave the place a last walk-through. It occurred to me that she would probably never return to this place she loved so much. When she was satisfied, we hurried together through the heavy rain to the Sartor's cabin to say our goodbyes. I was amazed at Mom's stoicism. She appeared strong and fearless. Even though her friend, Dolores, wept at the untimely farewell, Mom shed no tears.

"Ready?"

"Ready." And we began our long, slow trek into the remnants of Hurricane Belle.

Water swept over the winding country roads and the Thruway. We finally made our way down Venetian Boulevard, where the canal had flooded the houses south of ours. Luckily, our home had weathered the hurricane well, with the exception of a few fallen branches and the absence of power. Margie met us at the door. Mom kissed Margie and me and then swept past us to wash her face and change her clothes. "Let's go to the hospital to see Daddy."

"What are you doing here?" Through pain, Dad smiled up from his hospital bed.

"I'm back. Let's take care of you." Mom held his hand. I left them alone for a bit and later drove Mom home. They had decided to allow

Mom's cousin, a fine surgeon, to operate on Dad the following day to see exactly what was wrong with him.

I returned to my bayside apartment where, luckily, the water had risen only to the threshold. I was glad to be in my own place. I sat quietly for a long time, wondering what would happen now, gathering strength for the next surge.

Early the following morning, still without power, I took a cold shower and washed my hair. While I was wondering what to do without a hairdryer, the phone rang. Margie bluntly poured out words that made me go weak: "They operated on Daddy and found cancer covering the entire outside of his pancreas. There's nothing they can do. They just closed him up. He doesn't have very long to live."

Cancer. Nothing they can do. Doesn't have very long. To live. Oh God, please make it not be true. Please. Please. I couldn't stop the tears. I had to. I put cold water on a cloth and pressed it to my eyes. *No. Stop crying. You can't cry now. Mom needs you.* I commanded my eyes to dry, tied my damp hair up into a scarf and drove to the house.

"Where's Mommy?" I brushed past Margie and Bridget sitting at the kitchen table. "Mom?" I found her lying across her bed sobbing. "Mommy? You're going to be okay, Mom. You're going to get through this. We'll do it together—all of us. Come on. Do you want to go see Daddy now? He's probably awake by now. Let's go see Daddy."

I watched my mother rise from her bed with resolution. Something happened in her—some inner steel that she kept ready went into service. She rose, walked into the bathroom, washed her face, brushed her silver hair, put on her makeup, returned to her bedroom, and dressed up in a flowery print dress with matching heels. She wore a coordinating necklace and earrings. She looked stunning. She had decided in that moment that she was Marion Papagno, wife of Pat Papagno. She was a knockout, his knockout, and she would remain that for him. Any other tears were shed in private. My sisters and I followed our mother's lead; we dressed up to visit our father. We walked silently and stoically into the longest two weeks I'd ever known.

MY FIRST GOODBYE

WE SPENT MOST OF OUR TIME at the hospital. My sisters and I alternated keeping Mom company while she visited with Daddy. Mom seemed to be there all the time. Each day Daddy's health declined, and I could sense Death hovering in the corner of his room, waiting. It would take me years to sort out the events of these days.

One morning I navigated the twisting path through the hospital corridors to Daddy's room by myself. I paused at his door when I heard Daddy speaking Italian, something he never did. Prepared for some foreign visitor, I stepped into the hospital room to see Daddy poised toward the window—alone. He turned his head toward me. "Look who's here. It's Mary."

"Oh." I understood. When Daddy was a young boy in Italy, he had been given Mary, the only girl born into the family of seven boys, as his charge. They were inseparable. When the typhoid epidemic hit, Daddy, Mary, and their older brother were stricken. Daddy was the only one of the three to survive. His voice gentle and eyes cast downward, he had told me this story once when we were alone. He never mentioned Mary after that. To my understanding, Mary was the one who would come for him when it was his time. For now he was still mine.

Little things that ordinarily would pass without thought became monumental. Daddy asked me to buy him some Polident. He wanted to clean the dental bridge holding the two molars the army took from him during World War II. I stood in the pharmacy, debating with myself over which size to purchase. Usually I'd get the large economical size, but this time I knew that Daddy would not live long enough to need it. I bought the smallest package I could find and left the store choking on my decision.

A year before, Dad had flicked an ash onto his tie, burning a tiny hole in the silk. He'd asked me to embroider some design to camouflage the damage, a talent I used to embellish friends' jeans and blouses. It still lay in my embroidery box; I'd never gotten to it. *Should I do it now?* I wanted to do everything I could for my father, but I knew that he would never again wear the tie. I covered the box and tie, but could not cover my guilt.

Mom and I often drove to the hospital together. Once when we left for home, I was driving the car out of the parking lot onto Merrick Road. Mom turned to face me. "What am I going to do?" She looked at me blankly.

"You're going to go on. You're going to be all right. We're going to help you. You're going to go on, Mom." I did not know where these words originated, but I heard my voice calmly reassuring my mother of her future.

Daddy's friends, so many of them, came to see him. One day Uncle Sam, Dad's youngest brother and the most devoted to him, came rushing into the hospital room waving two tickets to Mexico. "They have a cure there. I read about it. They take apricot pits and grind them up. It can cure you, Patty!" He was a man who could not face what was happening, a man clinging to a shred of hope in those tickets.

"I don't want him to leave. He can't go to Mexico." Mom spoke softly to Uncle Sam.

"You're killing my brother! How can you kill my brother?" He pushed Mom to the wall and held her there. Margie and Bridget pulled him away. Uncle Sam was crazed. Mom was stunned. She was counting on Dad's brothers for emotional support. She had never before seen the holes in the fabric of our family.

"It's okay, Sammy. It's okay." Daddy mustered enough strength to say the calming words. Uncle Sam broke down in tears and left the hospital sobbing.

The following day Cousin Clara, known in the family for believing and investing in bizarre money-making schemes, came to visit Daddy with great news of a cancer-curing macrobiotic diet. She brought an expert on the subject with her. They spoke with Mom giving her recipes to make for Daddy. Mom went home that day confused and struggling. "He always loved my food. I made good things for him." Her thoughts swirled as she stirred the brown rice and garlic that Daddy was unable to eat that night.

Days slipped by in interminable boredom with nothing to do but sit, and horror at seeing Daddy's life ebbing away. Two weeks after Daddy was admitted to Good Samaritan Hospital, I saw a neighbor who'd been too busy to visit until now entering the room. Instinctively I rose and blocked the door, protecting Daddy from the outsider. Dying is a private matter. "My father's dying today. He's not seeing visitors." I heard my voice saying words I had not prepared. I returned to the vigil that Mom, Carole, Bridget, Margie, and I had stood these long days.

At ten o'clock that evening, August 23, Daddy struggled to speak. "Go. Go home." He raised his head and directed words to each of us individually, "I love you." To the next, "I love you. I love you. I love you. I love you."

At eleven o'clock Mom phoned me. Calmly she said, "I just got the call. Daddy died ten minutes ago."

"Okay. Mommy, do you want me to come over?"

"No. Go to bed. Good night." There was resignation in her voice, and calm.

I don't remember if I slept that night or what I felt, but I knew that the world was not the same—was not right—and never would be again.

A VISION

I BOLTED UPRIGHT IN MY BED, overcome by nausea. I ran to the bathroom and vomited into the toilet. It hadn't been a *dream* that sickened me; that couldn't be a *dream*. I was *there*.

I was tall. And a man. I looked down into the eyes of my judge, a dark-faced man like me. We both wore soft tan animal skins, only he wore a feathery headdress and a flurry of clinking carved bone beads around his neck. He spoke a language I have never heard, yet there I understood his word and their impact. "Do you know what you did against our law?" he solemnly asked.

"Yes." I was unafraid.

"Do you have anything to say in your behalf?" He had been my friend, I sensed, and this was difficult but necessary for him.

"Only that I would do it again if I had to."

"Then, you know what I must do."

I nodded, and he raised his right hand to my face, placed his wide thumb into the corner of my left eye and gouged it out. Experiencing no pain but knowing that my life would be over soon, that there was no hope, I felt my stomach clench as his left hand rose toward me.

"What *was* that?" I asked my best friend, Sandy. I trusted her to hear me out without judging me.

"Well, you've been under a lot of strain. Your dad just died. It doesn't sound like a dream, though. Too real. I think you flashed back to a previous life for a moment."

"Maybe." I wondered about this event. Was it strain that brought on a peculiar dream or provoked a glimpse into another time and life? Sandy and I often discussed such possibilities.

I had accompanied Mom to the funeral parlor. "Follow me," the attendant said quietly as he opened the showroom door. There, rows of satin-lined caskets stared us down with the reality of our situation. The attendant pointed out the best model—a polished steel box, guaranteed watertight forever.

"Mom, Daddy loved wood. He worked with wood. The rosewood coffin is beautiful, Mom, and I think Daddy would like it."

The attendant lost his smile along with the sale of the most expensive item on the floor.

Later that afternoon I went to Sherry's, where I bought a black silk blouse. I'd wear it with my herringbone skirt.

I dressed and met Mom, Carole, Bridget, and Margie at the house. We drove together to the funeral parlor. Quiet. Controlled. A man, dressed in a black suit, led us over the deep green carpet laced with roses toward a room. He held the door open, and we walked in to see the coffin at the far end of a long expanse. Flowers everywhere silently watched us. As I neared Daddy lying there, I saw that his hair was parted on the wrong side.

It was during the 60s, and I was in high school. The uncles and aunts were visiting for coffee and cake. Uncle Sam walked in wearing a turtleneck and a medallion. "Look at me, Patty. I'm mod." Uncle Sam smiled broadly at his older brother. We all laughed and joked about "modifying" Daddy's clothing.

"Yeah, Daddy, how about a necklace or a paisley shirt?"

No one thought any more about it. After we'd all kissed our aunts and uncles goodbye, Daddy quietly confided in me, "Drace,"—his nickname for me—"thanks for changing my hair that day we bought my new clothes."

I thought back to that day when I'd pinned Daddy's hair in place and gave him his new style. I remembered his response at seeing it. "I like it. Here's the new me."

As if practiced, I reached into the coffin and swept Daddy's hair over to the other side. "Poor baby," I whispered. "There, now you look great, Daddy."

When we saw the crowds that attended the wake that afternoon, we had the director open the wall to a second room. People chatted comfortably because we'd asked that the chairs be placed in oval arrangements.

I don't think I'd ever realized how many lives my father had touched with his smile and good humor, his special quality of making each person feel as if he or she were extraordinarily important. Hundreds of friends and relatives visited to tell us wonderful stories about him. There was much activity and many people to greet. For two days, we celebrated Daddy's life.

When the funeral and lunch we'd had catered at the house ended, and the last guest left, we cleaned up and talked about the day. We sat with Mom and sipped coffee at the kitchen table, the silence pounding.

"Mom, 'you alright?"

"Yes. You girls go home. I'm okay." Her voice was hollow.

I don't remember much of what I did after that. I wanted to resume "normal" life. School would begin in another week. I'd be busy doing what I loved—surrounded by a new group of students. But each morning, when I opened my eyes and remembered, I knew that although it was probable that I would again be happy one day, the finality of Daddy's death would always linger.

DAN

SCHOOL BEGAN IN A FOG THAT YEAR. I resolved to focus on my students and my work. When I was in the classroom, I momentarily forgot the sadness of Daddy's absence and was able to get on with my life.

Dan, who had visited frequently while Daddy was sick, was taking up more and more of my time, and I was finding him somehow more agreeable than in the past. I'd broken off our engagement the previous January, as we were clearly not right for each other. I found him to be high-strung, and he thought I was complicated. I hadn't missed him during our time apart, but Daddy's words from his hospital bed stayed with me. "Dan's a good man, Grace. It would be nice if you two were married."

It was something Daddy wanted, and he knew what was best for me, I thought. Mom offered neither objection nor sage advice. She was too sad and distracted to think deeply about my situation. I'm not certain that she would have given it much thought even had Daddy still been alive.

In September Dan and I were strolling through the quaint streets overlooking Long Island Sound. Wood smoke scented the chilly air. The annual Sea Cliff Minimart, studded with craft vendors and specialty foods, was one of my favorite events. "Well, what do you think?" Dan stopped and faced me. His eyes gleamed with a sincerity I had not seen for a long time. "Will you marry me now?"

In that glimpse I saw a life for me. I would be whole—with a husband and a family. "Yes. Yes, I will marry you, Dan," I said, and in the late September sunshine, Dan and I planned a simple November wedding.

"I'm happy for you both," Mom said with a sincere smile. "Are you two staying for dinner?" Mom had always liked Dan. Most people did. His sense of humor and timing were of professional comedic standards. He was most comfortable with an audience he could entertain.

He'd found a cottage on an estate in posh Upper Brookville, and even though living there meant a seventy-mile round-trip ride to work for me each day, I was filled with visions of happy times sitting by its fireplace surrounded by pristine woods.

I gave notice to my landlord that I'd be leaving my apartment by the Great South Bay in mid-November, and we hired the clubhouse there for our wedding ceremony and reception. My girlfriend, Sandy, found a caterer who'd come in, complete with a white jacketed, red-toqued chef! We sent out invitations. I drove to Garden City, the home of the most elegant stores on Long Island. Saks Fifth Avenue's bridal department offered me a strapless champagne colored satin gown with slipover top. "On your first anniversary you can wear this without the top. You can go dancing with your husband, and you will remember your special day," the saleslady said encouragingly. *Dancing with my husband. My special day. Anniversary.* I was carried away in my pretty dream. I purchased shoes and a small beaded bag to match the floor-length dress. Sandy's mother crocheted me *la busta*, a bag in which to place cards at the wedding.

The whirl of anticipation and daydreams filled my time. I pushed away thoughts of Daddy's death.

Two weeks before the wedding, Dan and I were in the cottage giving the walls a fresh coat of paint. The phone rang. Dan answered. I could see his jaw tighten and teeth clench, a practice that was already wearing his teeth down at age twenty-seven. "Okay. Yeah. Next week? Right." He hung up and flatly said to me, "They've switched me to week on – week off. Don't say a word."

And I *didn't* say a word. But instead of day-boating, which in Dan's tugboat industry meant that he'd go to work each morning and return each evening, he would now leave on a Friday to spend the week on the tug and return the following Friday. I would be alone in the cottage in the woods every other week. I would drive thirty-five miles to work and then thirty-five miles back to an empty cottage in an unfamiliar town, with none of my family or friends nearby. I lurched blindly toward the doomed marriage, hoping somehow that Dan and I would make it work, even though there was no evidence that either of us had the skills or the support of loving family to help us.

It rained for our November 18th evening wedding. Our plan to have people sit wherever they wished backfired when Dan's mother and stepfather took the table away from my friends, Ewald and Waltraud. Dan's father and his straight-laced wife were civil enough. But during the "bride and groom cut-the-cake" event, Mom swooped across the floor and snatched the piece of cake Dan was about to feed me. "The Mother gets the first piece!" she announced as she pranced off to murmurs from the crowd.

Afterward we drove up to Massachusetts for a weekend. We almost missed out on our ski honeymoon in Vail the following January. Colorado was having a snow-sparse winter, and Dan saw no reason to go if we couldn't ski, but I insisted.

And so we began our short, unhappy life as Mr. and Mrs. Through considerable pain, I learned that in my attempt to escape sadness, I had only created more of it.

WITHOUT DAD

AFTER DADDY'S FUNERAL, Mom picked up her life and lived it. I think her exuberance was partially for her own well-being and partially for us, her daughters. When I visited her, she made conversation about her work and mine. She tried out new recipes on me, and we discussed foods.

My sister Bridget made no objection when her husband, Joey, declared that they were going to move to Texas. They quickly sold most of their belongings and their house, and in autumn, so quickly after Daddy died, they left, taking my four-year-old niece, Sophia, with them. My heart broke to lose another member of the family—this time to distance. I'm sure Mom was downhearted too.

At Christmas time, I thought a complete break from tradition would be better than celebrating at Mom's house and feeling our profound loss in Dad's absence. I invited Mom, Carole, Margie and her husband, James, to join Dan and me at our little cottage in the woods for Christmas Eve dinner and sharing of gifts. Dan was scheduled to be home, and his presence would make the entire evening easier for me socially and emotionally. Everyone loved his sense of humor, and he would keep our festivities light and jovial.

I busied myself with the menu; it was not easy to prepare a party meal for six on two electric burners and a small, portable convection oven. My refrigerator was only waist-high, so Coleman coolers stored some of the perishables outside.

Light snow dusted the cold ground on that Christmas Eve of 1976, our first without Daddy. I lit the logs in the fireplace. As the room took on the orange glow of the firelight, I busied myself with all the last-minute details.

My family arrived with smiles and gifts. Dan had called earlier. As was common, his work schedule had changed; he had to dock a barge, and then possibly he could jump ship in Brooklyn. His presence at our Christmas celebration was iffy.

I set out the hors d'oeuvres and made whiskey sours for everyone. This had always been Daddy's role. We held our glasses and toasted, "To Daddy, who is always in our hearts!"

Before we could think too long, we began our usual banter. I started dinner which, because of lack of space, would be served buffet style from the chrome and glass sofa table. Some could sit at the small table for two, others could find places on pillows set upon the two-foot-high slate shelf that lined the glass wall, and anyone who wished could park on the rug softened by cushions. We watched the light snow fall onto the woods and down the hill through the glass wall. All was as quiet as a storybook Christmas.

Just before I began serving dinner, the door opened, and Dan appeared, snow on his head and in his moustache. He had hitched a ride from Brooklyn and made his way home. We all reveled in Dan's arrival, and for the remainder of the evening there were bursts of laughter from the small cottage in the woods in Brookville. I was happy to have my family together. I missed Daddy and Bridget and little Sophia—and I suppose even Joey, though he was the reason for my sister and niece's absence. Family became increasingly important as it diminished in numbers.

Mom made several other visits to the cottage over the next year. She was always ready for adventure, but she never saw the increasing anxiety between Dan and me. She had begun her new life and was forging headlong into it. She toyed with the idea going to Bermuda alone. She asked me one afternoon, "But what will I do there by myself? I don't like to eat alone, especially in a restaurant."

"Mom, when you arrive, you unpack. Then you walk around a bit to get an idea of the place. It will be dinner time soon after that, so you go back to your room, dress up for dinner and then go to the bar. Order a Dubonnet on the rocks with a twist. You'll like that, and it's not too strong. When you've finished your cocktail, ask to be seated for dinner. I guarantee it will be the only night you eat alone. Don't worry! You'll meet lots of people." I secretly prayed that my words would become reality. Mom returned from her first solo vacation with stories of good times and names and numbers of new friends. I laughed to think that I had taken on the role of mothering my mother. How strange, after a lifetime of her subtle, stinging innuendo that I was not worthy of being happily married, that I should teach Mom to be single.

Having conquered her fear of traveling alone, Mom was unstoppable. She took a windjammer cruise in the spring followed by a summer journey to Hawaii. The only thing missing for her was male companionship, and so she ventured out on a new crusade—to find a "boyfriend."

One of the girls at work told Mom about the widows and widowers dances. Without hesitation Mom made arrangements. She donned her fanciest dress and headed into Roseland in Manhattan, by herself, the following Friday night.

There she checked her coat and entered the ballroom. It was years later that I learned what had happened that night. It seems that another silver-haired beauty who was sitting with her friends caught a glimpse of Mom walking by.

"Hi," Palma called to Mom. "Why don't you sit here?" indicating the seat next to her. Every month thereafter, Mom and Palma headed to the ballroom for dancing and the ageless, timeless hunt for a man.

"I just liked her from the minute I saw her," Palma told me when we visited twenty years later.

With that ease, Mom, who had always focused all her attention on Daddy, to the exclusion of close girlfriends, acquired a best friend. Palma and Mom became a twosome who traveled and adventured together.

Since they both had boats, they took turns as "captain" when they went out onto the Great South Bay. They fished and clammed and laughed. I marveled at Mom's resilience.

Slowly she began to call me, not just to chat, but to ask if I'd like to meet her for dinner. I was amazed that I had such fun with my mom. I was no longer the target of her sardonic tongue. She became a friend.

She listened. She understood. She was interested. Even when Dan and I decided to separate, and I moved to the house in Sayville, she visited. She loved to spend time sitting on the front porch of the lovely old house, with me, just sitting, watching the world go by—together.

MY HOUSE ON MAPLE AVENUE

"YOU KNOW, IF THINGS DON'T CHANGE between us, I'll have to leave," I said diffidently. Dan didn't move but continued to stare blankly at the TV in our little cottage in the woods on the estate in Upper Brookville. "Okay then." And in the silence, I'd committed myself to leaving what was, for me, a very lonely place.

The following week was even colder than one would expect in January. We'd had another snowstorm, leaving Long Island, and especially Nassau County, with more snow than it had seen in years. Dan was away; this was his week *on* as first mate on the tug *Huntington*. I trudged up the small hill to my white VW Beetle, intending to find a new home today. Before I started the engine, the landlord met me and told me that the Long Island Expressway was closed due to the snow. I returned to the cottage with even more determination that as soon as travel was possible, I would venture out east to find someplace where there were people, friendly people, and a calm place to live, with no cold drafts, and more flowers than the meager daffodils that sprang up around the cottage in spring.

Two days later, with a copy of *Newsday* on the passenger seat, I braved the cold and snow and chugged onto the frozen tundra that was the LIE. Although the day was sunny and crisp, the myriad abandoned cars buried under snow and ice on the shoulders and exit ramps remained as evidence of the intense storm now past.

Hmm, Smithtown, that's closer to school, I thought as I passed under the exit sign. *I wouldn't have to make a thirty-five mile trip to work each morning if I lived in Smithtown. No, maybe a little farther.*

I found myself looking at an apartment in Patchogue. It was nice enough—a complex built around a small, man-made lake. There were holes in the walls that I was assured would be filled. There was electric heat. *Expensive.* The entrance to the complex was off a busy, sign-filled industrial road. I took the manager's card promising to let him know of my decision. "Hurry," he warned, "it won't last long." And as I gazed at the area on the way back to the parking lot, I could only ask myself, *Is this who I am? Is this where I will be happy in a new life?* Hope seemed to slip away, and I knew that I was totally alone.

Sayville's near here. Mom likes to shop in The Charlotte Shop in Sayville. I'll look there before I make my decision. So I backtracked to Sunrise Highway toward Lakeland Avenue heading south to that tiny town.

This is pretty. It's sweet here, like Lindenhurst used to be when I was little. I like the old houses here. I'd love to live in a house like Karen and Catherine's, and I dreamed a bit as I pulled up to Sayville Realty, a small, antique building in the middle of town. With the *Newsday* under my arm, I entered the stark room. It had a tall ceiling and a large black and white square tiled floor. A lone gray-haired woman stood up behind one of the big old oak desks. Her red lips formed a smile, and in a gentle voice she asked, "May I help you?"

"Yes, thank you." My voice began to quiver. Despair was catching in my chest tossing waves through my vocal chords. *Breathe,* I thought. *Don't cry. Twenty-eight-year-old women shouldn't cry so easily.* "Yes, I'm looking to rent the main floor of an old house. I'd like it to be in walking distance of town. I want to be able to do gardening, and I don't want the owner to live there. It should be in good repair. I'd like a washer and dryer, and I can't pay more than three hundred and fifty dollars a month including utilities." I seemed to spit out these words as if they had been rehearsed. My voice remained steady although tears crept into the corners of my eyes. I blinked them away.

"Why, we don't normally carry rentals," smiled the sweet lady whom I learned was Lillian Adams, "but I do have exactly what you described. How amazing." She looked at me as if I were some kind of apparition—that I had come by the knowledge of the house by preternatural means. "The owner of the house was quite old and after she broke her hip in a car accident, moved to be with her daughter in California. A local man purchased it as an investment. We just closed on it this morning. I don't even have the key, but I can show you the outside if you'd like."

"Oh yes, I'd like that." We walked to her car and drove around the corner, past several houses. There it was, a stately Dutch Colonial, the kind that a classmate of mine had lived in when I was in high school, the kind I so admired and envied. It had a very large tree, a copper beech, in front, and a screened-in front porch. "Does it look as good on the inside as it does on the outside?" I asked Lillian.

"Absolutely," she replied. "It's old, and Mae kept it up as best she could at ninety, but it's very nice. There's an elderly lady who lives upstairs. She's lived there for years."

"Fine, then." I handed Lillian a fifty-dollar bill. The deal was closed. I was the new tenant.

As if guided by angels, the house that I'd only dreamed about was mine. A year after I'd moved in, when I was ready to buy a house of my own, Lillian helped me look everywhere in town for *the one*. "No, this one doesn't face the right direction." "This one doesn't have a front porch." "This one doesn't have a wooden screen door that slams when it closes." Nothing was right. Then I realized that I was comparing all the potentials with the house in which I was living.

Cautiously over a period of months, I complained to the owner of things that needed to be fixed. This was my ploy to nudge him into selling the house, which he had not planned to do. "I'm having trouble with the water pressure." "The electrical boxes are all old and dangerous." "The cesspool is undersized and old; it could be dangerous." He agreed to sell me the house, for five thousand more than it its market value, but it was *my* house so I paid it. Mable, the old, upstairs tenant stayed on for years, her presence helping me to make the tax payments.

∞

This house on Maple Avenue has been very good to me. It is my comfort, my home. I take care of it, and it takes care of me. It has given gifts – a Civil War belt buckle I found under the front post, a ceramic beer cap with the letters GSP (amazingly, my initials), and a mother-of-pearl star I found in my garden. I have been here for well over thirty years and have vowed never to sell, although the value has gone up considerably in those years. I brought up my daughter here, and she loves this, *her* house. She knows that she can bring anyone here and be proud. Visitors are comfortable here, and even though there is nothing fancy about the house, the furnishings or the gardens, it is special—one of a kind—it is my house on Maple Avenue.

TREASURES

I CAN'T REMEMBER WHEN IT BEGAN. I think I have always had a love of old things. When I was very little, I rambled through Grandma's old house on 41st Street in Brooklyn, opening the top drawer of her chifferobe, sifting my fingers through her soft clothing, inhaling the clean fragrance of old wood and soap.

In high school, my best friend Betty and I happened to pass the Lindenhurst Historical Society's tag sale, an event rare in those days. I spotted a 1910 Singer Sewing machine covered in thick layers of dust. They wanted ten dollars for it, and I only had six. I begged the lady for the item, and when she relented, Betty and I managed to finagle the thing into the trunk of my Renault Dauphine.

Mom was definitely not happy with my find. "What do you want with that old junk?" she asked, but my love for my "new" sewing machine deafened my ears to her criticism. Careful cleaning revealed a like-new machine beautifully decorated with colorful scrolls across the shiny black painted iron, a worn leather belt which was replaceable for fifty cents, a decorative foot treadle, and mild abrasions to the oak veneer top. I asked Daddy to show me how to refinish the cover, and immediately a new avocation was born for me.

It seemed that wherever I went, I found auctions, sales, and even cast-offs that were beautiful. When I finally stopped moving around at age twenty-eight and purchased my 1927 Dutch Colonial house in

Sayville, I was thrilled and terrified at being a home-owner. I recall the realization that *now that I own a house, I have to furnish it!* With a budget that promised to cover little more than the mortgage and utility payments, I decided that garage sales were my best option. Little by little, and with a working make-shift shop in the garage, I refinished purchases made over years. I found an oak dresser in upstate New York and its matching washstand in Pennsylvania. I had difficulty extracting the rounded glass to remove green paint from the old china cabinet, but I did accomplish the job. The Hoosier cabinet began as painted white and now stands proudly golden oak in the kitchen. The classic black telephone on the desk works, as does everything in my house.

I have acquired old oak lamp stands and rockers, an authentic Art Deco bedroom set, oak-framed beveled mirrors, and a never-used hundred-year-old china set. On the way to purchase deck furniture, I came across a yard sale in Brentwood. It seems that the young lady's deceased grandmother had been a lace maker in Greenwich Village all her life. Her handmade lace curtains now frame my living room windows.

Not all my treasurers come from sales. I have found two carved, rosewood footstools, an oak desk chair, and two cushioned redwood arm rockers, all which had been put out for the garbage-men to collect. Once, while jogging on my lunch hour through the neighborhood of the school where I worked, I spotted a piece of furniture on the curb. I could tell by the side panels that it was old, and a peek inside the dove-tailed drawers revealed oak. I jogged back to school, drove the two blocks, and packed it into my trunk. Under the seven or eight layers of gaudy paint lay perfect golden oak. It is my lingerie chest that houses white gloves and lace collars, hundreds of vintage handkerchiefs, as well as my bathing suits, and dance apparel.

It seems I have cornered the market on black iron floor lamps, and have supplied Stephanie's apartment with two as well as having four in my house and two more in the attic. Ah, the attic. It is there that I have stored the furnishings for the cottage I will one day own. When Stephanie settles into a house with a family, I'll acquire a place nearby, and my finds will create another comfortable home for me.

It's not that I need to buy old things any longer; I simply love the quality, the richness, and the history each piece holds. Every one of my thirty-five rolling pins displayed on a rack in the kitchen has a story of the woman who baked for her family. Each 1940 colorful heavy cotton tablecloth stacked in a glass cabinet reminds me of the bride who waited for her soldier to come home. Each glass ice-box container and lid, which I prefer rather than using plastic, tells of a time before the influx of artificial materials. I have filled my home, my castle, with real items that not only serve a purpose well, but also have character and personality of their own.

I have come to realize that I have furnished my house as if I had purchased it new and had gone to stores in the 1920's, '30's, and '40's to outfit it. I sometimes romanticize that this is a throwback to a deep and happy memory of mine of a former life and time.

So if you happen to drop in for a visit at my house, I will serve you coffee made from beans that I will grind on the spot and boiling water I will pour over them, or perhaps if it is warm out, I'll make some lemonade out of lemons and water, sugar if you like or stevia from my garden. Maybe you'd like some chamomile tea, cold or hot, made from the dainty flowers in the herb garden served in one of many old teapots. I will offer you cookies I have baked out of real butter and unbleached flour and genuine chocolate, or warm brown bread I made earlier with yeast and oats and bran. If it's summer, I'll bake a pie and roll the dough that I put together with flour and butter and lard with a pinch of salt and fill it with blueberries from the dooryard garden. I'll select a rolling pin and think of the lady who used it before me.

My collections of old things are very precious to me. I find joy and peace in things of the past. When, one day, I have grandchildren, I'll show them hundred-year-old cookie cutters and marbles and books and games and piano music. These treasures are not gone. They live at my house.

GOODBYE, AGAIN

WHO CAN SAY WHY SOME LIVES go on and on while others are snuffed out early? There are no certainties in this matter—no rules or regulations. We dance. We play. When it is "our time," we pass and are finished here.

In the winter of 1978, while I was in the process of settling into my new home in Sayville, Mom met Michael at one of the Widow and Widower's dances. She asked me once if I thought badly of her for dating when Dad had been gone only a year. "Mom, I know you love Daddy," I said. "Everyone knows that. He's not here now, and you are. Live your life, Mom. It's okay."

She smiled at my acceptance and shortly thereafter invited me to join her and Michael for Easter dinner. Mom cooked. This was the first time I'd meet Michael, and I could sense that Mom was eager for me to like him. Some time earlier Margaret (as Margie now wanted to be addressed) had expressed her disapproval. I think she'd compared Michael to Daddy and found him lacking.

I arrived with Easter flowers and home-baked cake. Mom introduced me to Michael, who had arrived at the house earlier. He was average in height and build, and he had dressed neatly in a well-tailored suit and tie. Though thinning, his light brown hair was healthy and wavy. He was handsome, and I could see why Mom was attracted to him.

While Mom prepared each course, I conversed with Michael at the table. Now that he was retired, he enjoyed playing the piano in the morning, practicing golf in the afternoon, and visiting friends in the evening. I found him to be both genuine and interesting. I managed to whisper, "He's really nice, Mom, and handsome too," raising my eyebrows coyly when I delivered the French onion soup bowls to the sink. I knew well how disturbing it was to have family members reject the person you date. I never could please Mom until I brought Dan home.

Mom was happy. She dressed up to go dancing, to dinners, and even to vacation with Michael. Her world returned to normalcy at last.

Dan reentered my life. Having paid some "dues" he felt he'd owed me; he had now lived in the cottage alone for as long as I had, and he'd rethought the strain I'd been under living there in the woods so far from friends and family. With hope, he joined me in the Sayville house to see if we could mend the broken marriage, or more to the point, weave one together where none had been. He had quit the tugboat service and was now tending bar in Nassau County. He left for work an hour after I'd gotten home and arrived home in the wee hours of the morning, shortly before I had to rise to leave for the day. The prospects for growing together were unlikely.

Margaret and I spoke regularly on the phone. One day, though, after leaving her job in a doctor's office, and in her best dispassionate "medical personnel" voice, she gave the news: "Mom's had bleeding from her rectum for some time and never said anything. I brought her to the doctor. She has colon cancer. She's going into the hospital for surgery in two days."

My thoughts spun. How could this be? I'd been in this whirling mindset before, a little over a year ago, and was still reeling from Dad's death. *That's how these things end. But wait. Here there was hope. Colon cancer was treatable, even curable.* "It's not time to worry," my favorite character, Atticus Finch, would have told me. *Don't worry. It can't happen again,* I told myself. *Mom is strong. She's never sick.*

Counter thought pounced: *Daddy was never sick either.*

But colon cancer is not like pancreatic cancer. They can treat this. And so my internal debate continued.

After Mom's favorite cousin, Bobby, performed the surgery, he seemed uneasy to face my sisters and me with his news. "It was colon cancer. I removed the malignant section. That part is fine."

My heart leapt, but fell in a moment when I looked at Bobby's face. He was not finished. "The cancer filtered through her liver and is growing there. There's nothing I can do. She can go through chemo and radiation to treat it, but I don't know how that will go."

"How do you know it's cancer?" Carole asked innocently, looking for the flaw in this verdict.

Bobby looked defeated. "It's black."

Before Mom's surgery Carole had driven back home to Lindenhurst from Boston, where she lived, and we kept Bridget in Texas apprised of the situation. What we had to do now was get Mom to the oncologist and the radiologist. She was powerful and positive, and in her queenly manner, dressed elegantly for each visit. She continued her life as if nothing were wrong, nothing out of the usual were happening.

One Saturday Dan and I planned to go to the Fire Island Pines, a beach accessible only by ferry and known for its posh restaurants and amazingly wealthy clientele, both gay and straight. We found the place quite European and treated it like a quick (and less expensive) trip to France.

"Hey, Mom, why don't you come to the Pines with Dan and me? We'll have a great time. Be here by 8:30 a.m. and bring your lunch."

Mom needed no coaxing; she rang my doorbell at 8:30 sharp! We had coffee and drove the two blocks to the ferry. I was thrilled to see the gleam in her eye as we stepped into that land of exotic beachgoers and yachts. She loved it all!

We walked down the tree-shaded, narrow wooden "avenue" to the beach and set out our blanket. When Mom took off her shirt, I saw that she had indelible purple lines drawn across her back. "What are these?" I asked, touching the marks.

"Those are guidelines so that the technician will irradiate the same spot each treatment," she said matter-of-factly. Her words made me shiver.

When it was time for lunch, I carefully unwrapped lobster tails that had been leftover from the previous night's dinner. Dipped in cocktail sauce, these made the perfect beach lunch. Mom unwrapped her liverwurst sandwich and looked at me. "I'm not eating liverwurst!" she protested and reached for my lobster tail. I looked at the purple lines on my mom's back and was happy to swap lunches. "I love liverwurst!" I said with a laugh, and we all savored the day.

For as long as she could, Mom continued life as usual. She and Michael went out to dinners and dances, although she was not able to dance as energetically as before. They took a road trip out west and stopped to see Bridget, Joey and little Sophia at their Texas home. She told me that she'd gotten nauseous and vomited on the side of the road in the desert one day, but that, all in all, they'd had a great time.

Mom grew progressively weaker. She lost no hair. We could see that the chemo was not working. I offered to drive her to the oncologist's office one day where she stepped onto the scale to show me that she had not lost any weight. "One hundred and twenty-four pounds—the same weight as on my wedding day!" She was very proud of her trim figure.

When Mom and I decided that I should follow her car home one late afternoon, I could see that driving was difficult for her; she maneuvered very slowly and swerved several times. "Mom, why don't you try staying home from work for awhile until you feel better," I suggested after her friends at the office had called Margaret to say that Mom often fell asleep at her desk. They worried about her.

She agreed to stay home—"for awhile."

Margaret and I came to an arrangement: she would take time off to stay with Mom during the day, and I would drive to Mom's after work to have dinner and put her to bed. Mom never questioned our daily visits. She treated each day casually, as if nothing were wrong. I knew that she wanted it that way. The last time she'd visited me in Sayville, we chatted for a long time about nothing in particular. I finally found the courage to ask, "Mom, what am I going to do if something happens to you?"

Her answer was flat and deliberate. "Nothing is going to happen to me." I knew then that like Daddy, she had chosen a very private death. There would be no sharing of memories or imparting last wishes. Mom would fade away slowly, and we'd all pretend that nothing out of the ordinary was happening. And so we danced and smiled and prepared to meet Death again, only this time head-on.

LONG LIVE
THE QUEEN

"HELLO, CAROLE?"

"Yeah. Hi, Grace. What's going on?"

"You'd better come home now. Mom's not doing well."

"What do you mean? It's only the middle of October. The doctors said that Mom had a year to live—that she'd have until next summer."

"I know that's what they said, but Mom's not doing well. You'd better come home now."

"But I have work. Are you sure?"

"Carole, if you want to spend any time with Mom, come home."

I knew that she was trying to argue Death away. Margaret and I had watched the rapid decline and tried to gauge how long it would be. We called Bridget to come in from Texas. She'd arrive soon with Joey and little Sophia.

When Bridget appeared at the door a few days later, Mom asked, "What are you doing here?"

"I just came to visit, Mom," Bridget replied, and with that, all was understood without another word spoken. The four of us had come home to help our mother through her death.

We spent our days chatting, all of us. Mom moved from the kitchen to the TV room to her bedroom slowly and with our help. She showered with one of us in the bathroom to assist, helping her dry, cream, and powder herself. She was always clean and fresh and, as usual, beautiful. One day I came upon Mom sitting in the TV room. She had years ago lost her sense of smell, no doubt due to mixing strong cleansers together. She was striking matches, blowing them out, and sniffing the puff of smoke that remained.

"Mom, what are you doing?"

"I love the smell," she answered. She'd experienced one of the small gifts Death gives: a restoration before the body gives out.

My sisters and I cooked meals and served food around the table. We enjoyed being together but noticed that Mom ate very, very little and went to bed early. She slept soundly while the rest of us sat around the kitchen table and continued talking. Some nights Dan was there. Other nights, when he'd found a babysitter for little Sophia, Joey came to the table. It was always good to have different faces and new conversation. It was during one of the evening chats that Margaret confided something to us, "Dr. Samak told me that one of the possibilities with liver cancer is that Mom's abdomen may distend and her liver could rupture. In that case we'd have to rush her to the hospital. But he also gave me Percodan for her pain, so we might still keep her home until the end if that's possible."

We all agreed, but these thoughts gave me a surreal sense that I might have to witness more horrors than I could bear. Under the guise of normalcy, making jokes and small-talk, we continued to watch daytime television (something Mom had never allowed) and cook and eat and put Mom to bed. Having watched Daddy deteriorate within the cold walls of the hospital, and having nurses shuffling us in and out of his room, we had made a firm commitment that our mother would die in the home she loved so much. It was frightening for us, but we had resolve. I was twenty-nine years old at the time. Margaret, the youngest, was only twenty-five.

We never left Mom alone. We took turns sitting by her bedside while she napped in the afternoon and before she fell asleep in the evening. It seemed each of us had a special gentleness we brought to her bedside. I brushed Mom's hair gently, sweeping it back away from her face. She had always loved the sensation of having her hair brushed, and I remembered that, when I was a little girl, I had been delighted to be allowed to touch my mother's hair. Margaret talked to Mom during their times together. I could hear her voice in comfortable dulcet tones when I walked by the room. Bridget read to Mom. She sat and read and thought. Carole kept a journal writing in it intently during her vigil. As Mom weakened, Carole stopped coming to the table for conversation each night. "I'm not coming in there," she said once.

"Carole, come sit with us. It makes it easier. We're just talking," I assured her one evening.

"No," was her reply. "I don't belong with all of you."

Bridget, Margaret and I looked at each other wondering what we could do. Carole had always been aloof. It seemed to me that her lifetime of distancing herself from her little sisters had alienated her from us even now. She sat with Mom, waiting, waiting as if her need to be there at the last moment was crucial.

Ever since I was a little girl, I have loved to play the piano. Even though Carole's skill far exceeded mine, I found great peace in playing simple tunes. One day I found myself playing my old standby, "Moon River." I knew it by heart and played it quietly and slowly. Mom appeared in the archway of the living room and leaned against the wall while I completed my song. "It sounds so pretty," she said weakly to me.

"Thanks, Mommy. I played it for you." Then I walked her back to her recliner in the TV room. I didn't realize how much Mom appreciated my playing until after she'd gone. She hand-wrote into her will that I should have the piano.

People came to visit. Michael stopped in at the beginning, but as time passed, he simply phoned us to ask how Mom was doing. He gave her the privacy she wanted so that he would remember her as the vital, energetic woman with whom he had fallen in love. My sisters and I took turns leaving the house to be with others—to talk of ordinary worldly affairs that seemed so insignificant and unworldly at the time. My cousin, Clara, and best friend Sandy took me out one day. They were talking about diamond mines in Africa and other money-making schemes. I listened with no interest in something that seemed to be of no importance. After a while, we asked others not to come to visit, that Mom was comfortable but declining rapidly.

One day when I was preparing Mom for her nap, I fluffed the pillow and gently lowered her head and shoulders onto it. I pulled the sweet-smelling sheet and blanket straight. Then I sat carefully on the edge of Mom's bed and massaged her face, gently pressing at the arcs of her eyes, swirling at the temples, pulling back toward the hairline. I could feel her facial muscles relax, and she fell into the luxury of the moment. Her skin was still without wrinkles—amazing for a fifty-four-year-old, especially one in the late stages of liver cancer. She kept her beauty until the end.

"How do you know how to do this?" she asked plaintively.

"You taught me." The kind words slipped out of my mouth simply and without hesitation. I don't know where they came from. I had known the need for comfort, for tenderness, for love. I longed for the opportunity to have contact with my mother my entire life—a hug, a kiss. My mom had taught me inadvertently the need for gentle, physical caress by withholding it.

"I'm sorry," Mom whispered.

"It's okay," was all I could say at that moment. But for years and years I would think on exactly what Mom had said to me at that moment.

On Wednesday, November 8th, Mom ate ice cream with us in the TV room. We laughed and made ice cream jokes. On Thursday she ate nothing. On Friday she stayed in bed. Margaret called Dr. Samak, who came to the house to insert a catheter. Mom was no longer mobile.

"Margaret, Mom hasn't eaten since Wednesday," I whispered when she and I were alone.

"Do you want to bring her to the hospital where they'll hook her up to tubes and machines until she weighs forty pounds? That's what will happen to her."

"No, of course not."

"She can take sips of water. She's not in pain. Dr. Samak gave me morphine hypodermics for when she can't swallow the pills any more. She is aware of everything around her. Let's keep doing what we're doing," my little, medically-savvy sister explained.

On Sunday Mom could no longer speak. When she tried to get up, we all tried to calmly coax her into lying down. She seemed frustrated but relented. Later on Margaret quietly told Bridget, Carole and me that Mom had wanted to get up to use the bathroom.

With two bowls of warm water, a bar of Cashmere Bouquet soap, several washcloths and a towel, we quietly gathered around Mom's bed. We closed the door behind us. "Mommy's had an accident, and we're going to clean her and make her feel refreshed," Margaret said sweetly and softly. The four-o'clock autumnal sunlight drifted through small slats between the Venetian blinds, giving the room a warm, orangey glow. I took the cloth and wet it, soaped it, and began giving Mom the same sponge bath I had for the past several evenings. But now carefully, carefully, avoiding the catheter, I gently oh so gently swabbed freshness onto my mother's delicate regions. I couldn't speak. Margaret explained to Mom everything that we were doing as we did it. Tears escaped from my eyes and I blinked them away. I had become the soothing caretaker—the mother to my mother. It was the gentlest time we had all shared. Bridget, Carole and I left Mom cozied up in her fresh nightgown with Margaret murmuring soft words to her.

On Monday I noticed. "Margaret, the skin where you gave Mom her last shot is all red. Something is wrong."

"Her skin is breaking down. It's what happens."

It's what happens. . . . It's what happens. I watched my mother slowly ebb into another realm, and we continued our vigil.

On Tuesday I was sitting with Mom. I no longer brushed her hair, nor did I massage her. She was breathing shallowly, and my sisters and I took shorter shifts, changing places every half hour. Her skin had become translucent, which I learned later is the sign of the soul lifting from the body. "It's all okay, Mommy. You can let go. You can go, Mommy. We'll be alright."

I don't know if she had heard me. Late in the afternoon as I glanced into the partially opened doorway, I saw Margaret sitting by the bed weeping gently. I opened the door. "She's gone," Margaret said. "She just exhaled deeply and didn't inhale again."

I put my ear to my mother's chest and listened for a heartbeat while Margaret felt for a pulse. There was none. I took a mirror from the bathroom and held it up to Mom's mouth and nose. Nothing. I called to Carole and Bridget who quickly came into the room. "Mom's gone."

"Wait," I said to my sisters. "Carole, come into the kitchen." She and I went to the liquor cabinet and took out the bottle of Sambuca, our parents' favorite. We poured four small glasses and carried them into the bedroom on a tray, where we all surrounded the bed and took a glass. "The queen is dead. Long live the queen." We clicked our glasses and drank. It was as if we had rehearsed the movements of that moment for years, but none of us had thought about or discussed what we would do. It just seemed like the proper way to acknowledge our mother.

Margaret called Dr. Samak and the Johnson's Funeral Home on Wellwood Avenue. Dr. Samak had told us *not* to call the police, that they might not as be gentle with Mom as we would like.

Minutes later Dr. Samak arrived. We took him into Mom's room where he examined her and made out the death certificate. When he returned to the living room, he gave us all a hug. "I hope when I die, I have such care. Your mom had no pain. There is calm on her face. Ah, I hope that I have such care." And then he sighed, mostly for Mom.

The men from Johnson's arrived and gently carried Mom out on a stretcher. That's how she'd wanted to leave her home.

I would think of the things we said and did that came to mean so much to me, the simple things of those days when we were isolated from the world. The one thing I know is that people *can* change. People *can* see the damage they've done. And people sometimes apologize if they're lucky enough to have time and insight at the end of their lives. I also know that it has taken me many, many years to feel the weight of my mother's most important words to me. Slowly and through my own experiences, I learned the depth and importance of those most simple words and how they have set me free, those simple words of my dying mother, "I'm sorry." In answer I reply, "Mommy, I love you."

MY GIRL

UNLIKE MANY LITTLE GIRLS, I did not play with dolls, although I did have a few. Early on, when Daddy took me to a job site, I had one nestled into the crook of my arm. Mr. Taca, Daddy's builder, sweetly asked, "And what is your dolly's name?"

I remember being puzzled by the question. This was a doll, not a person. I hadn't given it a name. I squirmed against Daddy's leg, and he said something to Mr. Taca, and they both laughed quietly.

Another time later, some school friends took out their dolls to play. One announced, "Okay, this is my baby. Her name is Mary, and my husband's name is Bobby…." Whoa! Baby? Husband? When they took out the sheer curtains that one's mother had relegated to playtime, to use as wedding veils, I left the group and returned to my next-door neighbors to climb trees, ride bikes and go killy fishing.

Even though there were four sisters growing up in our house, we never dreamed of weddings, husbands or children. I suppose when Mom repeatedly told us that we would "never find a man as good as your father," we believed her. She even decided to have her lace wedding gown cut down, dyed lavender, and made into a dress for herself. The leftover piece was turned into a camisole. I remember Mom announcing, "What? Do you think I'm going to give my gown to you kids?" She never wore the dress. She said it didn't fit right. But after all these years, I have still kept the camisole, even though it never has and never will fit me. To

132

be a bride was never one of my aspirations. I simply figured I'd marry one day.

And so as time passed, I aspired to other goals: getting into college, finishing with a degree, attaining a teaching position, buying a house. When I achieved all these, I did marry—first to Dan, entering into a relationship doomed to fail before it began; and then to Stuart, whom I believed to be a nice guy who liked adventure as much as I. There was more to Stuart than I had seen in the beginning. He revealed his dark side to me in bits and pieces after we married. But before that marriage ended, we had had some good days. It was on a lovely day in July that I found myself sitting in the living room, saying to myself and to Stu, "Something is missing."

"What do you mean?" he asked.

"I don't know. I get the feeling that something is definitely missing. The house is clean, the laundry and ironing done, the gardens are weeded, the grocery shopping is done and the car is washed. There's something else. I feel emptiness. Something is missing, and I don't know what it is."

"Well, do you think we should have a baby?" he asked. We had never discussed children. I'd never considered that aspect of life. I sat amazed at the thought.

"What if we have one, and we don't like it?" I thought about the terrifying prospect of having a child who was like my sister, Carole, and shuddered.

"Well then, we'll sell it. A good baby could go for at least seventy thousand dollars," he said, and I chuckled at what I thought was a joke. Later I realized that he had been serious.

In exactly nine months, plus the two extra weeks my pregnancy lasted, my baby girl was born on Shakespeare's birth and death day, April 23rd. When I met Stephanie for the first time, her eyes were closed until I held her, and at that moment we connected. Her father and I sang "Happy Birthday" to her, and then she and I were off to our comfortable hospital room where we made each other smile for the next five days. I spoke to Stephanie about all the wonderful things I was going to show her. I sang her songs of adventure and delight. When I lay her on the bed in front of me and leaned down over her smiling and saying, "Hello

Stephanie," she smiled back. The nurse assured me that it was "only gas," but when her father came to visit, I demonstrated, "Hello, Stephanie," and there was the smile and no gas followed. After I repeated this five times and elicited the smile each time, we both knew that we were the parents of a happy soul.

Stephanie has brought me joy every day since. As an infant, she loved her bath and giggled and cooed while splashing in the water. Each day of her first two years of life, I gave her a full body massage after her bath until one day she said, "Mommy, no more."

"Okay, Steph."

Because I had to resume working when she was six months old, I found a fifty- year-old babysitter near the school where I was teaching, who spent the day making Stephanie laugh. After her first birthday, I moved Steph to a sitter very close to home who had a two year old son. They played, did arts and crafts and read stories each day. When Steph was six years old, that sitter moved away, and another woman, one who cared for several school age children in the mornings, miraculously materialized. At the new sitter's house, Steph learned to play Nintendo with other kids, polish her friends' nails, and get along as one of a group. Steph was a happy girl.

Steph loved books. Each night before bed I would read three different stories to her from the ten books I'd taken out of the library. I purposely chose books with great pictures and not too much text on each page. She would beg for more. "Okay, one more," I'd relent, trying hard to keep my eyes open, having done all the household chores after a long day at work. I found myself at the library twice a week in order to keep us supplied with enough books to read. I was inspired one day to ask for a library card for Stephanie. In that way we could take out twenty books at a time, ten on my card and ten on hers.

"Oh, I'm sorry," said the bespectacled librarian. "Your daughter can't get a library card. She has to sign her name in script, and obviously, she's too young."

My four-year-old and I went home with determination. I sat her at the counter and wrote her name in clear, plain script. "Okay Steph, practice this until you can write it." She loved the challenge and after about twenty minutes managed to scratch out her signature. Back to the library we marched, confident that we knew something the librarian did not. "We'd like an application for a library card for Stephanie," I repeated.

With a "hmpf" the librarian impatiently said, "She has to sign her name in script."

"Oh, Stephanie can do that," I said with a smug smile.

Hesitantly, the librarian offered up the application which Stephanie slowly and accurately signed—in script. "Well then," Ms. Hmpf went to her typewriter to fill out a card for Stephanie. Triumphantly, she and I danced over to the children's section to take out our twenty books, ten for me and ten on Miss Stephanie's new library card. Steph had been introduced to the power of thinking "outside the box."

Every time we visited Dr. Augustine, Steph's pediatrician, I would read the patient questionnaire aloud to her so that Steph could offer her own answers. She learned the words "gender", "insurance" and "marital status" early in life. It was not long before Stephanie, at age six, was filling out her own forms. I showed Steph where I kept the grocery list and instructed her to write anything she particularly wanted on the list. We also began to keep a journal. A coworker had given it to me at Steph's birth, but I had been far too busy to fill it out at the time. She and I would take turns each evening writing a note to the other and leaving the journal on the other's night table awaiting a reply. We did this for years, and my girl's maturing showed itself in her ever-constant thoughts, improvement in spelling and her change from printing to script.

When she was about seven years old, Steph insisted that she start picking out her own clothes. When we shopped, I would stand back while she carefully considered the apparel on the racks. I learned early not to comment in the dressing room either. Steph was perfectly able to decide and maintain her style.

When she was very young, Steph had no interest in watching television. I figured that her time at home would be better spent with me. In the kitchen, where I seemed to spend most of my time, she had access to the cabinet filled with Tupperware. She'd pull out bowls and tops and play while I stepped over her to make dinner and the next day's lunches. We seemed to be in a synchronized dance chatting constantly.

When she was ready, I monitored Steph's television viewing by offering her only movies that we watched together. One day, not long after her second birthday, Stephanie was playing with her toys while I viewed Shakespeare's *The Taming of the Shrew* twice making notes to use teaching the play. While I was preparing dinner that evening, Steph asked to see "The Kate Show," so I put the *Shrew* tape on for her to watch once again. At one point, she toddled into the kitchen to announce, "Of all things living, man's the worst!" and then stormed back into the TV room to watch Kate and Petruchio resolve their differences. That was my introduction to Stephanie's uncanny ability to pick out the one line that depicts the essence of every movie she sees, to the delight of her mother.

Steph traveled easily. When she was three, her father and I took her on a road trip to New Hampshire. There, at one of the restaurants we stopped in, a group of teens were dancing. Steph stepped out onto the dance floor to join them and called, "Come on, Mom!" but I was too shy to dance in front of strangers. When Steph continued to coax, but to no avail, the teens all crowded around her saying, "We'll dance with you!"

I have, over the years, confessed and apologized to Stephanie for missing that special moment with her. She thinks nothing of it, but I know it is a moment I will never recapture. Now whenever Steph says, "Come on, Mom!" I run to join her, no matter how silly it may seem or how shy I may feel.

When Steph was four years old, her father and I had divorced. By the time she was eight, I had saved enough for us to travel to Disney World for a vacation. Without a second thought, I plummeted vertically straight down a waterfall in a small cart at Splash Mountain seven consecutive times because Steph called, "Come on, Mom!" It was amazing!

Once after she'd grown into a young woman, my girl and I spent a Saturday in Manhattan. After breakfast and a cab ride downtown and shopping and lunch and a cab ride uptown and MOMA and beers at the Irish pub, Steph caught sight of the bicycle rickshaw man on the side of 7th Avenue, calling us to take a ride. "Come on, Mom!" and we were off and silly—laughing and cheering, the crowd we passed and our peddler cheering along with us! Steph let out her clear, bell-chime laugh and I joined her happily.

❧

My girl has enriched my life in myriad ways. I brought her up the way I wished I'd been raised. I was the mother I had wanted to raise me. I'd kept the promise I made to myself so many years ago, and I know that I was right. Freedom within boundaries, listening, empowering and "pulling rank" when necessary were the tactics I'd used, and thankfully, Stephanie is an amazing woman and my best friend.

LEN

I KNEW I COULD NOT STAY with Stu the way things were. He was a good father to Stephanie, but his unexpected mood swings with me were unbearable. Seeing my sadness, my sister Margaret casually said to me in one of our daily phone conversations, "You know, Stephanie will end up marrying someone just like Stu if you stay with him." That thought spurred me to seek help, which I found in my health insurance providers' directory. His offices were close to my school and I could afford the co-pay. Stu and I went to see Len together one evening, leaving Stephanie with a babysitter. That night my long, long journey to understanding began.

Stu and I entered the gray-toned office quietly. Len introduced himself. I saw a broad-shouldered man about my age, with black, wire-rimmed glasses and dark hair neatly pulled back into a pony tail. He was smartly dressed, and his demeanor was relaxed. He invited Stu and me to sit with him, and each of us revealed the "problem" as we saw it. Then Len asked me to leave the room so that he could talk with Stu privately. After about fifteen minutes, Len asked me into the office for a private conversation.

I suppose that I was hoping for a quick fix, a Band-aid, for hope, but

Len did not oblige. Calmly and straightforwardly he said, "Get away from this man as fast as you can; he will destroy you."

My mind reeled. "What about therapy? Couldn't we be fine if he had therapy?" I was desperate. Stephanie was only four years old. How could I manage on my own, and with a small child?

"It would take years of intensive therapy, and he'd have to be willing, which he isn't," was all that Len could offer me.

I sat in the car quietly while Stu drove us home. Shortly after that evening, I asked Stu to leave my house, the one that I had purchased on my own years before I'd met him. Len had agreed to see me; I needed help to get through the separation and divorce. I know that Stu's mean nature would make every aspect of his leaving difficult, and I was so weakened by his demeaning behavior that I had to learn how to stand up for myself. With Len's help I learned that and more.

I saw Len, off and on, for years, slowly learning how to gain emotional strength, which I had never learned from Mom. Through tears and sometimes laughter, Len patiently listened to me and offered his insights when I asked. After seeing Len and growing personally, I set out on my own, feeling as if I had graduated with a degree in myself. I would make an appointment about once a year, to go over things with Len, and we were always glad to see one another.

My life was happy. When Stephanie had graduated from college and was living and working on her own, I met a man with whom I fell in love, believing now I would have the partner I'd wished for to live out my life in joy. After a year, and we were by then engaged to be married, he betrayed me. I left the relationship. I knew the breakup was the right thing, but the sadness that accompanied his absence was palpable. I called Len, and again he was there for me.

Len pointed out the narcissistic trap I'd once again been lured into, and I learned more about the workings of people than I'd ever imagined, things I should have learned from my parents while I was growing up. I regained my balance and chose to keep my weekly appointments because I found Len was the only person I knew who would give me an honest and unbiased appraisal of my dealings with others and my feelings about the world. Our relationship has grown into friendship.

I have thanked Len many times for all he has done for me. I enjoy our conversations—sometimes about Manhattan shows, some about metaphysics and other times sharing stories of our dealings with people. Far from the businesslike therapist I first met many, many years ago, I now see the cultured man with a quick laugh, a love of the arts, who tells some of the best jokes I've ever heard. It's through Len that I have come from darkness and fear to light and understanding, from ever-burdening sadness to unshakable joy.

"Thank you" seems so understated, but from my heart, thank you, Len.

BUBBLICIOUS

BECOMING A SINGLE PARENT WAS TERRIFYING. I remember having said to Stu at the time when we discussed beginning a family, "Are you sure we're alright? I don't ever want to be in this alone."

Now I was in it alone—except that I had a little girl for whom I was completely and totally responsible. Because the child support was less than minimal, our outings were limited. I was delighted when Darla, an old friend with whom I'd recently reconnected, asked if we'd like to join her family and another on a week's vacation to Gilbert Lake in Oneonta, New York. The cost was reasonable since we'd stay in unheated, cold-water cabins with only a fireplace to ward off the chilly mountain evenings. Communal showers were available a short distance from the cabin, and we would share food expenses.

The anticipation of caravanning to the campsite, living in the wilderness and giving my four-year-old Stephanie time to bond with Darla's daughter, Elizabeth, and I with Darla, kept Steph and me chattering for weeks. "Should I bring my Barbie, Mom?" Steph asked. Dolls were not her idea of fun, and her one Barbie doll was her least favorite. But Steph knew that Elizabeth liked to play Barbie, so she added it to her bag of toys.

We started out very early in the morning, and Steph slept most of the ride upstate, leaving me to listen to the radio and follow Darla and Jim's car. The five hours slipped by, and we found ourselves in an Oneonta supermarket purchasing food for the week. I was surprised at Darla's aloofness as she slowly ambled down each aisle, casually shopping as if she were at home with nothing else to do. I was rattled when the bill was divided three ways among the three families, even though my family consisted of only two people while the others were made up of four each. But I said nothing because I didn't want to cause any friction.

Hours later we drove into Gilbert Lake State Park and were assigned cabins. Steph and I had a small two-bedroom with a tiny kitchen, a living room with fireplace, and a porch housing a toilet and sink. We excitedly unpacked and went outside to meet our friends for a walk through the park.

We were both disappointed to learn that Darla was planning to sit in an Adirondack chair outside her cabin for the remainder of the afternoon. Elizabeth had donned her roller skates but hadn't mentioned them to Steph before we left home, so Steph had not brought her own, although she would have loved to wheel up and down the roads with Elizabeth. Instead my daughter was left alone with a Barbie doll. We took the walk together. I had hoped that my only child would enjoy the company of other children during this vacation, but it didn't work out that way. Instead, Steph and I became buddies.

The week passed slowly. There were only two days that were warm enough to swim in the lake. The remainder of the time, Stephanie and I explored the woods, sifted through broken rocks for fossils and played board games on our porch. I did my best to be a playmate to my daughter. Elizabeth's coldness was a quality we had not seen before, and Stephanie's disappointment was evident.

Finally it was time to go home. Jim took the TripTik I had ordered from AAA, as he would lead the way. I was worried about Steph being bored on the long ride, because I could not entertain her and drive the Thruway at the same time. Happily, Steph fell asleep on the back seat as soon as we left, but an hour later she was awake wanting to know if we were almost home. I couldn't bear to tell her that our return had just begun.

Then I had an inspiration. "Steph, why don't you come sit up here beside me?" In a moment she had scrambled into the passenger seat and buckled up.

"Do you still have any of the Bubblicious left in the pack I bought you?" I personally dislike bubble gum and rarely offered it to my child. But vacation was a special occasion, and I was hoping some remained.

Steph dug through her right pocket and found a nearly empty sleeve of gum. "Yes, Mom, there are two pieces."

Thank you, God! I thought.

"Great! Take one for yourself, and give me the other." We carefully unwrapped our treats. "Now chew out the sugar." Steph looked at me quizzically but she began to chew. Jaws working, we smiled and savored the orange flavor. Then I went into action. I carefully noted the movements of my tongue, lips and palate. Steph had no idea what I was up to. I pulled down the visor on Steph's side of the car and slid open the mirror. I kept my eyes steadfastly on the road while instructing: "Okay, look at me. To make a bubble, first you have to form the gum into a ball." Simultaneously we rolled our tongues, forming what felt like perfect spheres. "Now you have to gently stick your tongue through the center of the gum while holding the edges with your lips." I didn't attempt this feat until I'd finished describing it, because doing both was impossible. Steph watched me with the intensity of a student learning the secrets of life. Eyes focused on the road, I demonstrated the formation. "Now you try it."

Steph watched herself in the mirror and tried to duplicate my motions. I took my eyes from the road for a moment to sneak a peak at my daughter poking her tongue through the gum but losing the edge at the last moment.

"Oh, it got away," she said sadly.

"That's fine. It's going to take a few tries. Do it again."

Slowly and with much care, Steph achieved the perfect configuration of lips, tongue and gum.

"Now, my darling, while holding the outside of the gum with your lips, very slowly blow air into the center of the gum."

Steph watched me as I demonstrated—at sixty-five miles per hour and intent on the highway—how to blow a bubble. She succeeded at creating a small one which quickly deflated.

"That was great, Steph!"

"Yeah, Mom, but I couldn't keep it. How do you keep it?"

"Well, once you have the bubble, you have to seal it up by pressing your lips together. Again I demonstrated the final step. This time I took the bubble out of my mouth and gently held it in my palm for Steph to examine. She noted the thinness of the bubble and the lip-prints on the seal, and with intense concentration she made one attempt after another while monitoring her progress in the visor's small mirror.

There was, during the entire ride, perhaps a span of thirty minutes when Steph put her precious gum aside to serve us lunch (which has always been her job on long car rides). Immediately following lunch, after swishing her mouth out with water so as not to add any particles of food to her "bubble-maker," Stephanie proceeded to practice and practice and practice some more.

As I turned left onto Maple Avenue, my little four-year-old smiled proudly through a mammoth bubble protruding from her sweet little mouth.

I have only a few fleeting memories of that first Adirondack vacation Steph and I took together. Ironically, the ride home provided us with the most fun we'd had all week. We still talk of the day long ago when Stephanie became a champion bubble blower!

MOMMY MAME

I DON'T REMEMBER ANY INSTANCE in my childhood when I had special time with my mom. Sometimes when I was alone with her in the kitchen peeling potatoes or setting the table while she cooked the family's dinner, there was no conversation between us, no sharing ideas or dreams or even relating events. Mom gave orders, and I obeyed.

My family did go on various outings together: to Radio City Music Hall in Manhattan at Christmastime, to the Bronx Zoo once, to Argyle Pond in nearby Babylon to ice skate, and frequently to visit family in Brooklyn or Valley Stream, but always we went as a family. That was Mom's idea of "togetherness." Mom, Dad, and Carole sat in the front seat of our car, and Bridget, Margie, and I in the back. I would have loved to spend a day with my mom, doing something together, just the two of us. I wanted her to listen to the stories of what I'd experienced in school, or what boy I had a crush on. I would have relished telling her what was going on in my life and what I thought about, but Mom was not interested in wasting her time in that way.

I never expected to be filled with the joy and the companionship I found in my child. Even before I met Stephanie at her birth, I was determined to teach this new person, my child, everything I knew. She was, after all, my experiment. I would raise her the way I wished I had been raised, fulfilling the promise I had made to myself long ago. I loudly sang the alphabet song to her when I drove my car, feeling my unborn baby dancing in my womb. I played Burgmuller's *Ballade* on the piano, my huge, pregnant belly nuzzled up against the keyboard and was not surprised ten years later when Steph mastered the piece in only a day, exclaiming, "Mommy, I feel like I know this song."

When she was six, I tickled her intellectual funny bone with the nautical alphabet. I gave her as much of the bell and whistle system as I'd learned on the tugboats long before I met her father, not knowing if she'd ever have need of it, but she understood each time I gave a double jingle when I backed up the car.

For years I had played the show tunes that I loved on our CD player, explaining the plots to Steph who listened eagerly. I regularly sang to her, "You're my best girl, and nothing you do is wrong. I'm proud you belong to me." I would pick her up and whirl her around the room. "And if a day is rough for me, having you there's enough for me."

Steph grew in personal confidence and maturity.

When Stephanie was seven years old, I eagerly agreed to join friends with their son to take the children to see Steph's first Broadway play, *Les Miserables*. Broadway had been financially out of reach for me in those early years of my single parenthood, but I was able to begin attending plays intermittently, and I looked forward to this particular play which I had not yet seen.

So moved was I by *Les Mis*, that when Steph asked for the sweatshirt sold in the lobby, I readily acquiesced. "Mommy, why are you so sad?" Steph asked as I tried to hold back my tears as we walked to *Café Un Deux Trois* afterwards.

"Oh Steph, it was so beautiful. It made me feel very deeply, and that's why I'm crying. I'm not sad, sweetie. That's what art does; it makes you experience emotions intensely, and when that happens to me, I cry."

Shortly after that, when she was still seven, Steph and I attended a performance of *Pippin*. It was then she decided that she had to "learn to dance like that." To this day we don't travel in the car together without singing the entire score of *Pippin*—complete with harmony, she and I.

Steph accepted my explanation of becoming tearful when my heart and soul are moved, and she experienced that deep feeling when I took her to see *Sweeney Todd* performed at the high school where I taught. Steph was only seven years old, and I had wondered if she would be able to grasp the plot and understand Steven Sondheim's complex music. She understood perfectly. Steph begged me to take her to see the second performance and her father to take her to the third and fourth performances of the show. We didn't know then that she would play one of the leads in her senior year of high school, or that later, when we saw *Sweeny Todd* on Broadway, it would be like meeting a macabre old friend.

Throughout the 1990s, Mayor Rudy Giuliani cleaned up Times Square in Manhattan. With the drug dealers and prostitutes gone, I was no longer afraid to take my little girl to Broadway. As I pointed out various aspects of the plays we attended, she allowed me to see things through her eyes too. My girl became my "Broadway partner."

A Funny Thing Happened on the Way to the Forum returned to the stage, and I thought a comedy would be a good change for us. We folded our coats and placed them one atop the other on her orchestra seat so that Steph could see the actors well. Her crisp, clear bell laughter rang out, stopping only when the play ended. Again, she asked me for a sweatshirt, and although I wanted to say yes, the shirt depicted nearly naked ladies with only small, pointed golden cones over their breasts. She certainly couldn't wear that to school—even in high school it wouldn't have been allowed. Her determined eyes convinced me to give in, so the following day I machine appliquéd clothing onto the ladies. Everyone was happy!

After that Steph and I took in as many shows as we could afford. We discovered the TKTS booth and ventured out to see *The Frogs, Cabaret, Jekyll and Hyde, Jacques Brel is Alive and Well and Living in Paris,* as well as Off Broadway shows like *Perfect Crime*. With each new show, I felt I should introduce Steph to a new dining experience. We hit Sardi's, the rotating restaurant at the Marriott Marquis, Carmines, La Prima Dona and Rossini's. I'd wanted a repeat of Rossini's, but Steph's attitude about dining was, "In a city with over a million restaurants, we don't eat at the same place twice!"

Our adventures extended to the London Theatre when we traveled to England. Steph was thirteen on our first visit, and later she chose London for her "Sweet Sixteen" celebration. Our rule was to alternate choices each evening. On our first visit, Steph chose *Perfect Days*, which we learned was Scottish when the play began. While the audience bellowed laughter, we struggled to acclimate to the language. After about twenty minutes, we were able to laugh along with the Brits, understanding the deep curlicues of the language. I was horrified to learn that the plot worked the theme of a thirty-something woman who, feeling her biological clock ticking, artificially inseminated herself with her gay friend's semen. "Oh Steph, please act like you're eighteen! I don't want anyone to know I brought a minor here." The actress did her lines upside-down so that the insemination would "take."

Steph laughed at me. She took the entire situation in stride assuring me that no one noticed her youth. "Besides Mom, what's the big deal?"

A great stop on both London trips was to the Globe Theatre where Shakespeare's comedies, *As You Like It* and *All's Well That Ends Well*, had us both leaning over the railing of the gallery, laughing so hard that more than once we lost our cushions—which cost a half-pound each to rent—onto the floor below. Dinner on these occasions was at the Globe Restaurant overlooking the Thames—Steph's one exception to the rule about dining twice at the same venue.

It shouldn't have amazed me that Steph's great surprise sixtieth birthday gift for me was an evening at *Wicked*. It was wonderful, and I realized that my best girl had grown up and was earning enough money to buy the tickets.

We attended the theater whenever we could. We stayed in Manhattan for a few days and nights breathing in the electricity of the place. I think I have successfully been the kind of mother I had intended. I took good care of my girl, helped her through difficult times, fed her vegetables, listened to her problems and joys, and nurtured her always. But I was also Mommy Mame. I showed Stephanie aspects of the world that not many children experience. She loves the theater, good food, and travel. And I know that, as the song goes, "If someday another beau comes along, determined to take her place, I hope he's resigned to falling behind my best girl!"

PUBLIC SCHOOL
FOR STEPHANIE

"MOM, MRS. RUEL IS ORGANIZING a trip for the Advanced Choir to go to Broadway for a show. Can I go, Mom? It will be in three weeks and will cost only $35. I'll use my babysitting money." I had never been to a Broadway show, and traveling to Manhattan was a special treat for me. I was sixteen years old and a high school student.

"I suppose so. I'll let you know tomorrow after I've thought it over. Now set the table for dinner."

I didn't bother asking Mom if she wanted to chaperone the chorus to see *It's a Bird, It's a Plane, It's Superman*. She wouldn't be interested. I was happy that she even allowed me to go, and it was more fun having my friend Betty's mom, Mrs. Gomez, be the parent joining us anyway. Mom never liked attending the concerts our Advanced Choir performed and usually found an excuse to miss them. She didn't ask me about the All State Music Festival that I was accepted into in my senior year either. She said I could attend if I found some other parent to drive me to the North Babylon High School where it was being held. By that time, when I had reached high school, I had no longer expected more from Mom. I had learned that I really wasn't important and that my insignificant activities at school shouldn't interfere with the family.

By the end of the fifth grade, my daughter, Stephanie, was ready for middle school. She'd mastered time management, hung out with a wholesome group of friends, and enjoyed learning. Because she would be changing classes for the first time, I thought through any problems that might arise for her so that together we might eliminate undue stress.

As a teacher in a junior high school, I'd seen scores of youngsters panic at not being able to open their lockers and get to class on time. To head off this predicament, I brought the Master padlock guarding our shed into the house, and there at the kitchen counter, I explained the mysterious workings of a combination lock: how important it was to bypass the first number when going to the second, how to complete the cycle exactly, and how to pull hard on the lock to open it. Steph practiced and soon was competent at the task. She and I attended the tour of Sayville's Middle School to familiarize her with the floor plan and how to gauge her walk from one class to the next. We joked with each other. "This is the room where the teachers go to scream and pull out their hair after class," I whispered to her at an unassigned door.

"No, Mom, this is the room where they take kids to interrogate them before pronouncing suspension." We struggled to keep our shoulders still while we chuckled silently.

Afterward, we shopped for any new clothes Steph felt she needed, although our conversations were usually backwards from the standard teenager-mother realm of interactions.

"Oh, Steph, that dress looks great on you. Let's get it."

"No thanks, Mom."

"But why not?"

"I don't need it."

"I think *I'm* supposed to say you don't need it, Steph, and *you're* supposed to beg me for it."

And so, without my imposing my taste in clothing on her, Steph developed her own casual, comfortable, yet very particular style of dress at that special time of her life.

The transition to each level of school was tranquil, and my girl focused on her classes, her friends and boys. All was as it should be. She was comfortable with herself and her situation. When Steph took part in the plays that her middle school put on each year, I helped by chaperoning and painting scenery along with her classmates. When Steph had reached high school, the students took over most of the workings of a performance. I found a way into the activities by assisting the makeup artist who transformed the students into characters. I was in the background, but I made sure that I was part of Steph's world. What she was doing was important to our family, and she appreciated my helping the group. I couldn't help thinking back to my school days and realized that I had changed the patterns and the thinking that had prevailed while I was growing up. I had created a healthy and happy family.

MUSIC

I CANNOT REMEMBER A TIME when there was no music. As a child, I danced while I cleaned the finished basement, my Saturday morning chore. There was an old hi-fi there, and I played all the 78s that had been Mom's when she was growing up. I thought it natural that a child should know all the lyrics to the hits from the 30s and 40s.

Upstairs Mom played her newer long-playing albums. She purchased one a week, carefully selecting from the myriad vinyl choices at E.J. Korvette's during her weekly shopping. Rhapsodies and swing, Sinatra and Lou Monte filled the house while I did homework and when the family gathered for dinner each evening. I also fell in love with Fred Astaire at an early age and never missed his movies when they were on television. I danced and sang along with Gene Kelly, too, and watched James Cagney portray George M. Cohan innumerable times each Fourth of July when Channel 9's *Million Dollar Movie* played *Yankee Doodle Dandy* continuously. I didn't simply watch the actors, I *became* the actors. Their story was my story, and I sensed their joy and sadness each time the movie played.

Classical music was reinforced in me during ballet classes. Either recorded or played on the piano, the masters accompanied my dance! Mom also offered me piano lessons until I was twelve years old, when I lost interest in practicing. Classical pieces ran from my brain through my fingers into the piano. We were one!

The music program in the Catholic elementary school I attended consisted of singing a song in front of the class once a marking period to attain a grade. But when I entered the public school system, I was introduced to my first choir. In my junior year, I decide to join the Girls' Chorus. Under the guidance of Mrs. Giorgiana Ruel, a strict perfectionist, I learned several techniques: not to sing through my nose (by pinching my nostrils closed while I sang); to eliminate breathiness (by holding a candle in front of my mouth while I sang, trying not to blow it out); to listen to those around me; and finally, to blend my voice with the chorus (by holding a finger over one ear). It was hard work and sometimes frightening when Mrs. Ruel lost her patience. She would peer over the upright piano, her straight black bangs revealing dark brown eyes piercing arrows at us. I survived and was accepted into the Advanced Mixed Choir the following year.

Singing with male voices was exhilarating. I learned the harmony to classical, secular, and sacred pieces. That year I made it into the All-State Choir. We all did! What's strange is that I still remember all my parts from that year, so well ingrained was our music, and so serious was Mrs. Ruel.

In college, singing with the Women's Glee Club each Monday night, and Tuesday and Thursday afternoons, was a stretch for me. The other girls were very talented, and most of our music was difficult. I learned that in addition to giving concerts periodically on campus, we also sang with Men's Glee Clubs from other colleges at home and away. The pieces we sang with them were classical in nature, frequently masses, and always with several movements, guest soloists, and large orchestras. What wonder! What delight!

I never joined a sorority in college. The Women's Glee Club was, instead, my group of sisters, my friends, my travel mates. It was the highlight of college for me. Later in my freshman year, Mr. B asked me if I would join the Jongleurs, a woman's octet that specialized in madrigals and some popular pieces. I could hardly believe that I'd been asked to be in this most impressive group. My voice was not that of a soloist. I learned later that my blending skills and rich tones were what made me desirable. Somehow I made the group sound better.

With the Jongleurs I traveled even more and sang in a multitude of venues. The madrigal, a secular Renaissance a cappella song intended to be sung by a small group, is absolutely strict in timing and dynamics. We had such fun singing songs as "The Nightingale" and "Though Philomela Lost Her Love." In such as these, each musical part sang a different "coo-coo" or "fa-la-la-la," filling the air with the sound of birds or laughter. Mr. B often included jazz numbers in our repertoires, and so I learned and loved the swoops and stylization of familiar pieces.

Because of my experience with the Women's Glee Club and the Jongleurs, I learned that I could anticipate the fugue, my favorite section of a piece, and that I knew the dynamics of a Gregorian chant. I had been immeasurably enriched by being a member of these singing groups.

Then life happened. I graduated from college, found a job, bought a house, married, and raised a child. Music was confined to playing the piano when I had a moment, but there was always music in the house. This was a way of life for me and then for my daughter, who also played the piano, who danced to classical (and hip-hop and jazz), who watched *Mary Poppins* thousands of times so she could do "Step in Time" perfectly, who joined the chorus, and loved music. Stephanie discovered as she grew up that not every house was filled with music. "Billy's house always has sports on," she remarked one day. "There's no music, Mom."

When Steph was in the fifth grade, her school put on a tribute to various musicians. Stephanie was given a solo; she was Scott Joplin. That was the first time I saw her public performance ability, and I was shocked at her aplomb and talent. After that day, I never doubted her skill at entertaining others.

Steph took organ lessons as well as piano during her middle school days. In her recital that year she played Bach's Toccata and Fugue in D minor flawlessly for a packed house. The audience was so moved by Bach, and the fact that it was played by a young girl, they rose to a standing ovation shouting "Bravo" and cheering for my girl. I was astonished at her musical accomplishment and felt utter pride.

Throughout high school Steph sang in the chorus and was awarded parts in the plays. She became an actress, a dancer, and a singer. At her senior concert Steph invited me to join her, her chorus, and the high school alumni in singing the Hallelujah Chorus. There was my girl next to me, a young woman, poised and graceful, who actually liked singing with her mom.

Steph grew up, graduated from college, and took a position in an impressive company. It was then that I took a chance and auditioned for the esteemed Babylon Chorale. Even though I experienced shocking stage fright at my audition, I was accepted. The night before my first concert with the group, the conductor suggested that we might sing Handel's "Hallelujah Chorus" as an encore. Concert night she led us into the piece, and then without warning, stopped conducting. We just sang, and what beautiful, perfect, joyous sounds poured forth! It seemed to me that anyone who has ever sung in a serious group knows the "Hallelujah Chorus." It's axiomatic. Once you've learned it, you just never forget it. "It's like riding a bicycle," said my new friend Ellen who stood next to me. And somewhere in that moment of superior joy, in my mind's eye of long, long ago, I could see Giorgiana Ruel's bangs and her eyes peering over the piano, smiling at me, and I could sense my daughter, my Stephanie, singing next to me, all for the love of music.

WORDS I REMEMBER

I AM A WORDS PERSON. I love words. I am careful how I use them, and I am easily hurt by one or two applied carelessly by a less word-conscious individual. It seems to me that I remember spoken words far more clearly than memories experienced through my other senses. I keep spoken words carefully in my heart.

Growing up, whenever I'd asked Mom how I looked, she answered, "You look alright." If I challenged her tyranny, she would answer, "Don't start," without ever listening to what I had to say or trying to understand how I felt. I suppose that it was her effort to make my father feel special that she repeated the words, "You'll never find a man like your father," to my sisters and me over and over through the years. These words remained long into my adulthood when I had to re-learn kinder words about myself.

Now I do make an effort to set aside unkind and unjust words, since they do not serve me and tend to make me sad. Those that remain are usually pleasant and positive, friendly and funny. There are others, though, that touch my heart and soul, the words that I choose to remember always: the words of my daughter, Stephanie. They seem to define our relationship and the course my life has taken.

Surprisingly, Stephanie's first words were not "Da" nor "Mom," but "Up Up," the phrase her father and I used regularly when lifting her. She was an active girl, and "up up" was her get-up-and-go signal. As a toddler feeling deeply, yet not having the words to express her feelings completely, Stephanie looked me in the eye one day, held my hands and said, "Mommy, I love you *too much!*" Her words expressed the emotion simply and completely; we repeat the uncomplicated phrase to each other quite regularly, even now that she is an adult, and it has the same impact today as then.

Her father and I first introduced Steph to the tricycle when she was three years old. She'd race past our house and then the neighbor's, coming to a decidedly unsafe screeching stop. Although I suggested many times that she slow down, speed was her passion. One day, as Steph skidded toward my legs, stopping just in time to prevent a crash, I admonished her and suggested that she take more care. "Mom, you're disticable!" she pronounced, as seriously as a hanging judge giving his verdict.

"Don't call me disticable, Stephanie," I said, quietly amused by the mispronunciation Daffy Duck had taught her in a recent cartoon, amazed that a four-syllable word was in her active vocabulary, but far more hurt by the fact that my girl really meant to tell me that I was "despicable." Even today, there are occasions when to my daughter, I am "disticable," and she tells me so. My reaction is still the same.

During her middle school days, Steph and I were invited to a classmate's family party. There the adults mingled and chatted while many of the girls pretended to be on stage with the real microphone provided by the hosts. Each took her turn pretending to be emcee of some fantasy-TV show. When Steph was given the mike, she assumed her take-charge position, thanked everyone for coming to "the show" and surprised me by announcing, "And now, ladies and gentlemen, MY MOM!" Caught off-guard, I quickly became the humble guest and expressed gratitude for being asked onto the show—then quickly retreated. Her proud face her words still ring in my mind. What admiration this young lady had for me!

As college age approached, there was much involved in finding just the right school for Stephanie. She made many of the phone calls for information from the various colleges and universities she thought might be right for her. One day I had to leave the room to privately consider what I'd witnessed; I'd overheard Stephanie interviewing a director of admissions. She was succinct, calm, and professional employing many of the phrases and questions I had used in my own business dealings. My girl was emulating me, the greatest form of flattery, and I was so grateful.

When she left home for college, I got no weepy "I miss home" phone calls. All Stephanie's conversations were filled with excitement and enthusiasm. I missed her terribly but felt delight that Steph was happy and confident. One particular phone conversation remains in my mind: "Thanks for teaching me organization, Mom. When all the other kids are wasting time looking for things they need, I know exactly where everything is. I look in the logical place, where I'd put it—just like you said." There was another call: "You know, Mom, how when I kept you waiting, wasting your time, your punishment was making me sit at the counter practicing cursive writing? Well, now everyone tells me I have beautiful handwriting! Thanks, Mom!"

Graduation from university was approaching. Steph had already accepted a prestigious job. We stood in the kitchen, our favorite room in the house, and I said to my girl, "Steph, you have so many wonderful qualities: you're confident, honest, clear thinking, straightforward, happy, good company, intelligent and kind. It had taken me well into my forties to even begin developing many of those qualities. I'm so proud of you."

With not a pause, nor a thought, nor a blink, nor a start, Steph offered me words that rendered me speechless: "You didn't have the mother I had."

My girl, now a woman, frequently e-mails me from work. We share ideas, problems, and solutions, recipes, and plans. I told her of my recent weight loss. Her answer: "Woo hoo!!!!!!! We will soon celebrate your skinny minny-ness with another shopping trip! I'll go through the collection [of clothes] to see what I have for you. A certain collared button-down from Ann Taylor comes to mind. I'll see what else!"

"Steph, you're so much fun!" I shot back.

"I get it from my mom!"

Stephanie and I will spend Mother's Day together. We will chatter like spring birds do in the early morning. Among the thousands of words we'll share, I know from experience that many will go into my special collection of Stephanie's loving words, the ones I keep carefully in my heart and will always remember.

BRING ON THE DANCER

I DON'T REMEMBER EVER wanting to be a princess or a bride. I never played "Mommy" with dolls. I don't remember playing with dolls at all. What I wanted more than anything was to be a dancer!

Across the cold tile floor of our finished basement, I mimicked Leslie Caron's steps as I watched her dance in *An American in Paris*. I studied Martha Graham's philosophy of the dance when I caught her special show one Saturday afternoon. In my heart and soul I was a dancer, and I suppose Mom knew that because she sent me to dance lessons, though none of my three sisters were offered the opportunity. Perhaps they never had the passion.

First I attended Miss Joanne's school in West Babylon for tap, ballet, acrobatic lessons. I was in second grade then and took my pliés, relevés and arabesques very seriously. I loved the smell of the wood floors, the resin powder box, and the sweaty ballet slippers and leotards. Mom eventually tired of the weekly drive, so my career was retired by fourth grade. I suppose I was relieved to be spared her complaints about the time wasted by the ride there and back and the endless recitals which she begrudgingly attended.

In fifth grade, by virtue of incessant nagging, I won the battle for more dance lessons. Mom delivered me to a new school held in the lower level of a house, where my teachers were an older lady who did not dance at all and a younger one who demonstrated new steps. The two of them led the class at the barre while doting on one teenage dancer—their protégé. Her talent was tap-on-toe which was, in my opinion, unfeminine, ungraceful and definitely not dance! I didn't like this school, and when Mom made me use my five-dollar birthday gift from Aunt Alice to pay for my lesson one day, I decided to end my dance career. But I never lost my love of the dance.

Much later, when I'd been teaching for three years, I learned that the Eglevsky School of Ballet, renowned for its high quality staff, held adult classes. With much trepidation I enrolled in the evening session.

The familiar smell of ballet hit me when I entered the studio. I was at home. Quietly, very aware of being the "new girl," I donned my slippers in the dressing room and took a place on the floor. There is a hierarchy in dance, of which I was well aware. As the new person, it was my place to quietly join in, to observe, to defer to the better and especially to the best dancer in the class. The teacher was a handsome young man who took the Long Island Rail Road from Manhattan. We young women argued to see which one of us would pick him up at the Massapequa train station and drive him south to the school on Merrick Road. Because we were all enamored of him, we worked very hard. I progressed as a dancer and moved up in class rank.

The following summer, "Mr. Handsome" landed a job on Broadway, and so Mr. Eglevsky himself taught the class. He was a great teacher, but old, and we were disappointed to have lost our young man. Our sadness was displaced by awe when Fokine came to teach us the following autumn. Although he was in his late seventies and walked with a cane, this icon of the dance, dressed in his bedroom slippers, would often drop his cane and spin across the floor, culminating in a perfect leap. Under Fokine's tutelage, I became an accomplished dancer. I was strong, lean—able to elevate either leg slowly and hold it parallel to the floor in perfect balance. I could turn, glissade, and jump. I now stood in the front row.

One of my dancer friends, Shelly, invited me to a party and introduced me to the crowd, a group of assorted artists. "This is Grace. She's a dancer." My heart leapt at the moniker. It fit me. I was a dancer!

Soon after that Shelly and I went into Manhattan where we purchased standing-room-only seats to *Pippin*. So enthralled was I with the play that I barely noticed I was standing. When Pippin sang the words, "I've gotta be where my spirit can run free/ Gotta find my corner of the sky," I felt the overwhelming need to find my place in the world. Surely I was not destined to be an English teacher forever. How dull that would be! There must be a place where I could be something more, something sparkling—something artful. So my search for my life's meaning began.

Twenty years seemed to slip by. We would celebrate Stephanie's seventh birthday that April. The winter had seemed endless as usual with promise of nothing new, when one of my favorite students approached me after class one day. "Ms. Papagno, would you like to come to see me in a play next weekend?

Without hesitation I told Dave I'd be delighted to see his play. "What show are you doing, Dave?" I was curious.

"*Pippin*," the clear-eyed, tall, slim student announced.

My mind spontaneously jumped to the theatre teeming with sensuous dancers slithering up the sides of the proscenium, Ben Vereen directing the young prince toward his destiny. "Oh, I love that play, Davy. What part will you be playing?"

"I'm Pippin, Ms. Papagno. Will you bring Stephanie?" My students had heard as many stories about my daughter as she had about them, and Davy Davis was her favorite seventeen-year-old heartthrob.

"I'm sure I couldn't keep her away. Count on us to be there!" With that, the plans were set.

The Saturday of the play was gray and drizzling. I was hoping that the young players wouldn't damage my memories of the original Broadway production too much. Steph and I found places on two folding chairs in the middle of a small auditorium. *How are they going to pull this one off?* I wondered.

At exactly 2:00, the curtain rose, and the narrator began singing, complete with sensuous dancers slithering up the sides of the proscenium. I was immediately transported to the middle ages as King Charlemagne sang of wars, and Pippin complained of smells in the dungeon. At intermission, as if waking me from a dream, Steph's words jolted me out of my thoughts of life and love. "Mom? Mom! This play is great! Mom, I have to learn how to dance like that!"

Prince Pippin discovered the meaning of life, the ensemble sang its grand finale, and Steph and I congratulated Davy and the cast. The afternoon had been more than entertaining; it had been transformative.

After school the following Monday, I drove Steph to the Sayville Dance Center where she enrolled in ballet and jazz dance classes. She was a natural dancer who picked up the essence of the art and added character to it. One day she came home and said, "Today we learned a *forte*, but I'm not sure just how to do it yet, Mom."

"Well what aren't you sure of? It goes like this: *arabesque, tendu, glissade*, and jump!" I demonstrated the explanation.

With open mouth, Steph gasped, "How did you know that, Mommy?"

"Hey, I've been training to be your mother forever!"

Steph eventually surpassed the expectations of her dance school and switched to Releve Dance Studio and the American Ballet Center in nearby Bayport. There, Stephanie exploded into a vibrant dancer who shone onstage consuming the attention of the audience with her talent and charisma.

Whenever Steph and I traveled, there was an occasion where her dancing became a focal point. On our windjammer cruise in the British Virgin Islands, some passengers arranged with the captain for Stephanie to dance to *Amazing Grace* while the sails were being lowered one evening. On the islands of Barbados, Aruba, and the Dominican Republic, Stephanie danced the limbo so well that she hovered as low as the professional. She won awards on all the islands. We jokingly called her the World Limbo Champion. Whenever we took long car rides, we invariable played the *Pippin* sound track, singing along and harmonizing with one other.

Life runs in meaningful patterns which we don't usually notice until one has come full circle.

When Stephanie was fifteen-year-old, the Sayville Players performed *Pippin*. She didn't expect much in the way of a role because she was a freshman, but we were thrilled that she would at least have a part in one of our favorite plays.

At that splendid performance, thirty years after attending the original *Pippin* on Broadway and wondering what my life's meaning would be, I watched my girl, my Stephanie, the lead dancer in the play, and I knew in a moment the circle was complete. Raising this young woman, this dancer, was my "corner of the sky."

MICHAEL, THE ANGEL

WHEN STEPHANIE WAS SEVEN YEARS OLD, I found my way clear to taking our first real vacation, a five-day package to Disney World, my first visit there as well. Steph was thrilled that she would finally see the characters she'd grown up loving; I couldn't wait to witness her delight. We had no idea then that what would impress us most during that holiday was neither the magnificent meld into the magical world of cartoon characters, nor the sweet surroundings of surreal imaginings, but one person's simple act of kindness.

Once settled into our room, we quickly hopped onto the tram heading to The Magic Kingdom. We were sitting across from a woman about my age and her two young children. We smiled at each other and shared our excitement at being in the best place in the world for kids.

I am certain that I was even more awestruck than Steph walking down Main Street, USA, seeing Cinderella's Castle in the distance. Stephanie, though, could not get her fill of Splash Mountain. I was lulled into a sense of false security by Br'er Rabbit and all the characters sweetly singing, "Zip-a-dee-doo-da, zip-a-dee-ay/ My, oh my, what a wonderful day," when I saw the cliff over which our car was about to tumble. My heart raced while my stomach fluttered weightlessly, and I screamed during the entire free fall! I'd barely caught my breath when Steph grabbed my hand, called, "Come on, Mom," and began running toward the entrance of the same ride so we could once again career over the waterfall.

Damp from seven rounds of Splash Mountain and the mist that had begun to fall, we headed back to our room on the bus. Here we met the same woman, Judy, and the children, this time with a younger couple. It seemed that the youngsters were her grandchildren, the young couple her daughter and son-in-law. We chatted a bit more and then got off at our respective hotels.

At dinner, I was not at all surprised to see Judy with Jim, her husband; Michelle, their daughter; Michael, her son-in-law, and the grandchildren. It seemed that we were destined to get to know each other, for we turned up simultaneously at the same places over the next few days. Eventually I learned that Michael had been diagnosed with cancer and did not have very long to live. He was weakening daily. Judy and Jim had funded this adventure to Disney World so that the young children would remember their father having fun with them. I tried not to judge Michelle, who seemed bitter at having her world turned upside-down, facing impending widowhood and being a single parent. Michael was slim, handsome, intelligent and funny. He quipped one-liners that made all of us laugh while we rode the tram the following day.

The light mist that fell on our first day had gradually evolved into rain, but Steph and I carried plastic ponchos with us everywhere, so our enjoyment was not hampered by the bad weather. On our last day, the rain cleared and so we traveled poncho-less by bus to Fort Wilderness for the *Hoop-Dee-Doo Review*, a Wild West show and dinner. By this time we were not at all surprised to meet Judy, Jim and their gang there. We were happy to see them and told them that we'd be leaving the following day.

Having forgotten all troubles, and having thoroughly enjoyed the show, Steph and I were suddenly taken aback to see pouring rain when we stepped outside. It was very dark and the puddles were deep. It must have rained the entire time we had been in the windowless playhouse.

People disappeared into buses. We buttoned up our sweaters and scampered to the stop for our hotel's bus. It offered a three-sided, roofed canopy. We sat, huddled together, and hoped that the wait would not be long—but it was. Very long. The wind had picked up and was swirling torrents of rain over us. The roof offered no protection from the sideways slaughter of the cold deluge.

Suddenly the pelting stopped. It was as if the rain had suddenly ceased, yet we could see it falling all around us. I took my head away from the protection and warmth Steph and I had found in each other and saw Michael looming over us as he stood on the bench behind us. Wearing his poncho, he'd spread out his arms and, angel-like, covered Steph and me, shielding us from the storm. This frail, dying man cared more about helping us than himself. I smiled up at him and he down at me. We said nothing. Michael canopied us for nearly forty-five minutes.

I have often thought of the heroics of this brave man, long gone, his wife probably remarried, his children grown. I hope they know what a great man their dad was—what a compassionate and giving and funny man, this Michael, the angel.

THE NEW
NORTHVILLE

MANY YEARS AFTER MY PARENTS DIED, when Stephanie was eleven years old, we packed some clothes, put our two kayaks on top of the car, and headed up to the country haunts of my younger days when Daddy worked at the race track in Saratoga. Steph was thrilled to pick out three books on tape, and I made sandwiches and iced tea for the ride. While I drove, Steph read directions, navigating us over highways, and always kept a book playing. Half-way to our destination, she served lunch, carefully placing a napkin over my lap and handing me my sandwich. I laughed when, one time as we left a rest area to resume travel, Steph said, "Okay, Mom, let's put the movie back on." We loved our books.

Finally crossing over Northville Bridge, I felt like Rip Van Winkle. After so many years, nothing had changed. We checked into the Flip Inn on the Great Sacandaga Lake and drove around the town. We stopped at the Lakewood Cottages and saw Eleanor, but learned that her husband, Heinz, had passed. She'd sold off the cottages to various families, but she invited us to walk down to the beach so we could see the lake and my old camp. Just being there again made me miss my parents and the happy times we'd spent. Luckily, Steph was there with me and wanted to go for a rowboat ride around the lake. Her eyes glowed in the soft sunlight, and I knew that she felt for the place what I'd always felt there:

tranquility, reverence for nature, and a sense of free spirit. When I asked Eleanor if she knew of any other camps we might rent, she suggested Nancy Bailey's at the far end of the lake, cautioning me that Nancy was very particular about her guests.

Steph and I drove to Nancy's Pine Point Camp, which consisted of two cottages on an immense lawn rolling down to Northville Lake. Nancy's house, long yet not imposing, sat behind the cabins nearer to the street. She was working in the hairdressing shop attached to her house when I gently knocked on the door.

"Well, hello," Nancy said with a wide-eyed smile.

"We're looking for a camp to rent. Eleanor Pritze recommended you to us. My parents and the Pritze's were friends for many years."

Nancy scrutinized us for a moment. "I've got nothing this year, but I could git you something for next summer," she said, her upstate accent noticeable.

"That would be perfect!"

Steph and I had dinner at the Sportsman's Club chatting excitedly about next summer's vacation.

The following day, after riding our bicycles and kayaking up the Sacandaga River, Steph and I packed up to return home, biding our time until we would become "regulars" at Northville Lake.

We were ready the following August. I had packed bedding, towels, mats, beach toys, and food into boxes. I discovered that Steph had an uncanny knack for loading the car, fitting everything we needed into it perfectly, and with no squeaks or rattles for the ride. We looked like exiled beach gypsies leaving Long Island for the Adirondacks.

After unpacking, we walked to the lake where we met the family that would reside in the other cabin: Nina and Neil with their son, Logan, and daughter, Miles. While Nina and I settled down on the lawn to read and sun ourselves, Logan, Miles and Stephanie found their way to the lake, jumped in, and were headed toward the raft which was anchored a little way out. Their laughter and squeals at being tossed into the water, being king of the mountain, and being dunked lasted all afternoon. After dinner we all gathered in jeans and sweatshirts to make a campfire and roast marshmallows. Neil taught us about the Perseids, meteor showers that were plainly visible in the darkness of the wooded

Adirondacks, and so we all lay down on the lawn to watch nature's star-studded show. Every few seconds a shooting star would sail across the dark sky and a collective "ooooh" flowed from all of us.

On other days, the three kids swam, with the aid of untrustworthy floats, to the short end of the lake, where they could swing off a tree into the deep water. We watched them and delighted in their laughter, even when Logan forgot to let go of the rope swing, hurling himself into the massive tree. Happily, he was not injured. At night, Logan, Steph, and Miles would stay up into the wee hours working on a jigsaw puzzle and then sleep until noon, which was fine with the adults. We were all on vacation.

Early in the mornings, I would awaken, put on my walking clothes and sneakers, and trek onto the roadway, up the steep, steep hill, around the back end of the lake, past my old Lakewood Cottages, up the small bridge road (where I could see our camp housing my sleeping Stephanie), through the village, across the spillway of the big lake, and back home. The few drivers who passed me always waved, and as I came full circle, the poplar trees on the edge of the spillway seemed always to applaud me with their tiny flapping leaves.

The saddest part of our week was when, on our last morning, the three new-found friends had to say goodbye. They did it silently. They stood, knee-deep in the lake, facing outward, just standing and breathing it all in—enough to last through a year until finally we'd return to our lake. And we did return—for many years.

Stephanie spent her teen summers with Logan and Miles swimming, boating, and simply having fun at Northville Lake. Eventually, Logan went into the service, Stephanie traveled with her school, and Miles married. We adults returned to Northville for a few more years, but for me it lacked enjoyment without Stephanie, so I said *goodbye* to my camp and my little town in the mountains.

I may return someday, perhaps with Stephanie and her family. We'll have to scout out a new campsite; I heard that Nancy Bailey passed a few years ago. We will have a new place in an old town with new people, but always there will be joy in Northville.

FINDING GRACIE

NICKNAMES FOR MY DAUGHTER came to me naturally.

At first, Steph was "My Darlin'" and "Sweetie Pie." She grew into "Petunia" and "Doll Face." By the time she was in middle school, I'd listed thirty-three monikers Stephanie answered to, and all were based in love and tenderness. Each of her Christmas presents were gifted to one or the other of her myriad names (and all *from* a selection of yuletide characters). One day, Stephanie curiously asked, "Mom, what are your nicknames?"

"Oh, I don't have any. My dad used to call me "Drace" when we were alone, but my mother didn't allow me to have nicknames. When my friends called me 'Gracie,' she'd inform them sternly, 'Her name is Grace.'"

"Oh, is that right, Gracie?" was Steph's answer, and with a twinkle in her eye, she took it upon herself to let all her friends know that that was how they should address me. Except in formal occasions, Steph introduced me as, "My mom, Gracie." It took me a little while to get used to the idea of being "Gracie." I had to give it a lot of thought and finally realized that "Gracie" was the funny part of me, the aspect I'd never relaxed into before Stephanie showed me how. By attaching the name to my joy and sense of humor, I accepted it and was comfortable wearing it.

When Steph was sixteen years old, we took a windjammer cruise around the British Virgin Islands. As we were presenting our passports upon boarding, a group of teenagers grabbed Steph informing her, "You're with us!" Without so much as a "hello," she'd been accepted into the group which ate, swam, and adventured on the boat all week. I found friends in a couple from Tennessee, Tim and Christie, and another from Washington State, Glen and Janet. Tim told me his most wonderful love story, how he, a builder love-struck at first sight of Christie, who worked in the town planning department, brought different plans into her office weekly just to see her. It worked. Glen and Janet were about to be married. He was a nuclear physicist and she a professor. They sang together at karaoke contests making quite a bit of money simply having fun.

Both Steph and I were enjoying the week immensely. When we docked at the island of St. John, I finally got some time with my daughter. Steph and I walked to Cinnamon Bay Beach, where she quickly caught up on her sleep by taking a nap, and I caught up on conversation when I saw Tim and Christie there. They invited me to have a beer with them. After a while, Tim in his slidy Southern drawl asked, "Another beer, Gracie Lou?" With that, Steph's head popped up awake and alert. "I like it!" she announced. And so a new nickname was born.

Since then I answer to a long list of happy "Lou-inspired" names such as Loula, Loulabelle, and Louella, as well as Gracie and Gracie Lou.

I had told Steph when she was a little girl that a well-loved child has many names. It took me a long, long while, but finally, it was my daughter who gave me all the nicknames it took to make me know I am well-loved.

JOY

SUSAN SIDESWIPED A POTHOLE trying to avoid a blisteringly fast car coming up on her, which flattened her tire and, she later found out, bent her wheel. Worse than that, the wheel could not be replaced in time for her to make it to the conference in Boston for which she had already paid. I volunteered to drive, and so my dear friend and I embarked upon our first overnight adventure together.

What remains most vividly in my memory of that weekend jaunt occurred during dinner on the first evening. We'd wandered up to the North End where Italian restaurants lined the narrow cobblestone streets. Arriving without a reservation, we'd followed the host through a labyrinth of rooms and hallways until we were seated at a cozy booth near the swinging doors to the kitchen. There were others in the room— couples, friends, and a casual wedding party.

The happy young man who had been hired to play Italian songs on his accordion came into the room and entertained us for a while. He continued his minstrel's walk throughout the restaurant and later, while we were eating our dinner, he stopped at a table just outside our small room. He began playing Bon Jovi's *Livin' on a Prayer*, noticeably *not* Italian. Susan, in good cheer, began to sing along with him.

> Whoa, we're half way there
> Whoa, livin' on a prayer

Take my hand and we'll make it—I swear
Whoa, livin' on a prayer

The young woman in the next booth joined Susan in song. Then the entire wedding party began singing. I saw the waiter hurriedly nudge the musician, pointing to this lively audience. Fingers dancing, the performer entered the room, whirling in the midst of the "Whoa, we're half way there." Everyone was singing—in full voice! The room was enveloped in the joy of the moment. We cheered. He laughed. The owner grinned in delight.

Walking back to our hotel, I thought about what had taken place in the *Cantina Italiana*. It was unrehearsed, unspoken, spontaneous joy.

Joy has been on my mind a great deal since then. I have concluded that it is joy that gives true meaning to life. Joy is the instance of delight we find in a moment. For me it is the satisfaction in a job well done. It is not hearing the music, but that moment when the music touches my heart. It is the recognition of the soul in a flower. It comes in the deep inhalation of salty air on the beach watching sunlight dance on morning whitewater. It is the good fortune in finding a book that was "made for me" in a rummage sale or turning on the television to find a very old, favorite movie just beginning. It is a moment of sheer interest in what Stephanie is telling me when we snuggle on the sofa, each at our own end, feet in the middle.

Glimpses of where I learned joy come to me while I slowly make my way through my gardens, picking weeds, deadheading flowers. The first gardens I played in were those my grandmother had planted, and later, my mother's. Very few people were interested in perennial flowers then, but my mom had a way of coaxing even difficult plants into growing. Roses covered the front of the house where I grew up. Guests sitting in our back yard would delight in the perimeter of flowers showing off their splendor.

Mom gave me a houseplant when I first left home on my own. It died. She gave me another. Then another—until finally one lived. When I purchased my house, Mom had already passed, but I remembered what she had taught me in her yard. I have, it seems, always been surrounded by gardens. My mother, without knowing or trying, gave me this gift.

My dad worked very hard at fixing up our house. It seems that I was always his assistant, holding tools, handing him each nail as he was ready for it. As a result, I grew up knowing the names and uses of carpenters' and plumbers' tools, a realm usually reserved for men. I have been able to deal with simple repairs in my house and have helped many of my friends. My father gave me this gift.

In describing the difference between her friends' houses and ours, when she was growing up, Stephanie explained, "There's always music in our house, Mom." I hadn't really given it much thought. Playing the family piano Mom bequeathed to me is soothing. The stereo is usually on, playing a CD and even vinyl at times. In the kitchen, I am tuned into the local radio station.

I think back to where I learned music. Of course, it was in the basement playroom with the old records. I sang, danced, pretended while doing my chores. Mom bought a hi-fi record player when I was a little girl. It was state-of-the-art at the time. She played classical pieces, Sinatra, and frequently we would all cha-cha in the living room with Dad. When she cooked and baked, Mom had her kitchen radio playing. Our house was alive with notes and melodies and voices. My mother gave me music.

For most of my childhood my mother was like a drill sergeant. She had four daughters up and out, having made their beds, in bathing suits, each with something to carry: a duffle of towels and another of sweatshirts, blanket, lunch cooler (the contents of which she had prepared the night before) and thermos of cool juice. Everyone was present and accounted for in the car—and off to the beach by 8:00 a.m.! Even if the day were overcast, if the weatherman promised sunshine, Mom would have us all waiting in sweatshirts on an empty beach. We went to the beach every weekday in the summer. I learned to know and love both bay and ocean, saw them in their brilliance and in their bad moods. I found joy and peace at the seashore. My mother gave me this.

When Daddy came home from work, our family always sat down together at dinner. This was a firm rule in the house where I grew up. Daddy's peace and tranquil way of talking made family time special. Sometimes he read stories to my sisters and me on the living room couch where we all snuggled together, feet entangled. Although infrequent, these were quiet and loving times, and so I read stories to my daughter every night when she was a little girl. These are some of the sweetest moments we shared. Without knowing it at the time, my father gave me this gift.

Most of the time in this life, we are all "livin' on a prayer." What gets us through and keeps us coming back for more are the moments of joy. We don't know when they will come. The best that we can do to instigate joy is to create the arena for it. For me, most instances of joy I experience have been given to me by my mother and father, who, as they told me—and I believed them—did the best they could. And I know that despite everything, I have come to a magnificent place of understanding, acceptance, and contentment. I'm more than "half way there" and I continue with the help of joy.

ABOUT THE AUTHOR

Grace Papagno taught English in the secondary school system where she introduced her students to wonderful literature, great writing, and tough love. She is an avid gardener, a member of myriad local organizations, and a favorite Italian cook to those who have the good fortune to dine in her kitchen.

Printed in the United States
By Bookmasters